THE [illegible] AN

CW01629122

The Urban Christian

Raymond Bakke
with Jim Hart

MARC Europe
Evangelical Coalition for Urban Mission

British Library Cataloguing in Publication Data

Bakke, Ray
The urban Christian
1. City churches
I. Title
261.8'3 BV637

ISBN 0-947697-61-6 (MARC Europe)
0-946842-02-7 (ECUM)

Unless otherwise noted, Scripture quotations in this publication are from the Holy Bible, New International Version Copyright © 1973, 1978, 1984, International Bible Society. Published in Britain by Hodder and Stoughton. Used by permission.

MARC Europe is an integral part of World Vision, an international Christian humanitarian organisation. MARC's object is to assist Christian leaders with factual information surveys, management skills, strategic planning and other tools for evangelism. MARC Europe also publishes and distributes related books on matters of mission, church growth, management, spiritual maturity and other topics.

ECUM (the Evangelical Coalition for Urban Mission) is a partnership of agencies of similar background and outlook working in varying aspects of urban mission. The member groups retain their separate identities while the Coalition seeks to express and service wider aspects of urban ministry. The Coalition is concerned with the application of the Christian Gospel to urban issues which, since the formation of ECUM in 1980, have become of central social, economic and political importance.

Copyright © 1987 by Raymond Bakke. First Published 1987. ISBN 0-947697-61-6. All rights reserved. No part of this publication may be reproduced or transmitted in any form or by any means, electronic or mechanical, including photocopy, recording, or any information storage and retrieval system, without permission in writing from the publisher. This book is sold subject to the condition that it shall not, by way of trade or otherwise, be lent, re-sold, hired or otherwise circulated without the publisher's prior consent in any form of binding or cover other than that in which this is published and without similar condition including this condition being imposed on the subsequent purchaser. Typeset by Furlonger Phototext Ltd, Victoria Chambers, Fir Vale Road, Bournemouth, Dorset BH1 2JN and printed by Anchor Brendon Ltd, Tiptree, Colchester, Essex CO5 0HD for MARC Europe, Cosmos House, 6 Homesdale Road, Bromley, Kent BR2 9EX.

Contents

Foreword by Rt Rev David Sheppard 7

Introduction by Jim Hart 11

Map of World-class Cities 12-13

Definitions 14

Chapter 1 From the Cowsheds to Chicago –
A personal journey 15

Chapter 2 The Lord Is Shaking Up the World –
A review of world population and urbanisation 28

Chapter 3 We Never Did It That Way Before –
The churches' failure to respond 45

Chapter 4 A Theology as Big as the City –
An outline for urban theology 62

Chapter 5 Build Decision-making Like Muscle –
Exercises with an urban congregation 88

Chapter 6 Into the Community –
Being an effective urban pastor 111

Chapter 7 Worship, Work and Witness –
Aims and methods for an urban church 131

Chapter 8 In the School and On the Street –
Bringing up a family in the inner city 162

Chapter 9 Networking the World –
International urban ministry 183

Chapter 10 Do It Yourself –
Equipping your church for its task 192

Bibliography 205

Index 207

Foreword

by Rt Rev David Sheppard, Bishop of Liverpool

Many Christian readers have long known about individual heroes in urban priority areas. What is new in recent years is that Christian voices in these areas have challenged the whole Church about its priorities and about its ways of believing and of doing theology. Ray Bakke was pastor of a Baptist church in Chicago for ten years. Since then he has studied and taught urban ministry, while remaining firmly rooted in Chicago. *The Urban Christian* is written out of his life's experience.

One of the most misleading trends of the present moment is to pin labels of 'traditionalist' or 'liberal' on every Christian. Ray Bakke defies such labelling. His basic theology is orthodox, biblical, evangelical. From that theology, worked out among poor people in a great city, comes a whole series of radical challenges to the Church and to the whole of society about racism, poverty and injustice. He will not allow 'sound' evangelicals from comfortable suburbs to tell him that he should stick to the simple, clear presentation of the Gospel to individuals and avoid social involvement. To Bakke these are not in opposition, but are two sides of the same coin. Throughout the book there is an insistence that the Church has good news to offer; but that the poor will not listen to the Church unless they see it standing much more firmly for justice.

Like many clergy, he began his ministry with programmes; slowly he learned that the salvation of the world would not come through programmes and campaigns. The Body of Christ needs liberating from all demanding Church programmes; instead he encourages us to learn about 'networking'. Christians need to build their bridges of friendship, so that their own networks begin to flourish. That rings true to me. Much Church life would change if clergy and ministers took his advice and spent one day a week 'investment time', networking their communities. Cities are made up of series of networks, and the art of urban living is to discover how to enter into the giving and receiving which comes from belonging to them. We need all the allies we can get! *The Urban Christian* is very helpful in spelling out the extent to which networking is possible. It breathes a generous spirit. Certainly there is evil to be resisted, but the Church is not to retreat into a ghetto, cutting itself off from the many unexpected allies whom God will give us in the city. He includes all the other clergy, unless they will have nothing to do with him, 'peer professionals' in service agencies, undertakers, barmen, businessmen, politicians, teachers. He wants us to have one arm round the Community and the other round the congregation.

In the midst of this co-operative spirit the limitations of authoritarian leadership become very clear. At a recent meeting of clergy and deaconesses working in urban priority areas in Merseyside the point was made that it will take at least twenty years to establish strong church life in unchurched districts. The right conclusion was drawn that it will therefore take longer than one person's ministry. We clergy must learn to be less individualistic, more willing to listen and learn from those who are already there, and to build on the good beginnings made by predecessors.

Ray Bakke knows about issue-based community action; he rejects some of its forms as being too adversarial. He is prepared to go looking for allies in the business community, trying to bring about changes in policies which result in 'red lining', refusing loans, insurance and services to inner-city areas.

The same co-operative spirit touches what he has to say about other faiths. There is the remarkable story of the Pentecostal Christian in Surabaya raising money and spending six months helping poor Moslems to build a mosque. There is the sad comment of a Christian woman in East London, 'I felt there was no Good News for the Bangladeshis, when Christians hated them, or wanted them to go.'

If Christians are to learn from the painful experiences of churches struggling to live in urban priority areas, we need some at least to learn how to do theology within that urban setting. That means not being so busy or so alone that no reflection can happen on the rich experiences God gives us in the city. There are many clues about how to produce Christian reflection in Ray Bakke's book. It can be both an inspiration and deeply educational.

David Sheppard
Liverpool, 1986

Ray Bakke has produced, in conjunction with World Vision, a three-part video series entitled *The City for God's Sake*. These videos may be hired from MARC Europe, Cosmos House, 6 Homesdale Road, Bromley, BR2 9EX, for a nominal fee.

Introduction

Ever since modern cities emerged in the Industrial Revolution, Christians have experienced difficulties in sharing the Good News with their inhabitants. Today, vast urban agglomerations feature on every continent, and house about half the population of the world. (See map on following pages.)

Many Christians have a vague idea that the Bible is a rural book, and that God's children should leave Sodom and live in the suburbs. Cities are believed to be especially sinful, and their inhabitants unusually hardened against the Gospel. Even if this were not so, how could Christians expose their children to the corruption of the city? Ministry there is for celibates only – or is it?

Raymond Bakke robustly refutes all these beliefs both by the example of his family and in his teaching in theological seminary and worldwide consultations. The appeal of his teaching is that his theory derives directly from his personal spiritual journey – his experience as an urban pastor and his family life in inner Chicago. This book therefore weaves together aspects of his autobiography and his teaching on urban ministry. The former legitimises and illustrates the latter. One of the key issues for the urban Christian, both in Britain and America, is how to live a 'Christian' family life in difficult urban environments without disadvantage to one's children. His experience here is practical and inspirational.

The material which follows has been gathered from consultation transcripts from Copenhagen, Oxford, London and Liverpool; from Dr Bakke's unpublished manuscript 'The Urban Pastor in the World Mission of the Church'; and from an article in *International Bulletin of Mission Research*, Vol. 8, No 4. This book is designed to appeal to the average reader who is not necessarily technically qualified – urban pastors, Christian workers and leaders of all kinds, young people and church members. For this reason, bibliographical references have been largely omitted, but a list of popular, easily available books has been included (p.205).

Jim Hart
Liverpool

WORLD CLASS CITIES

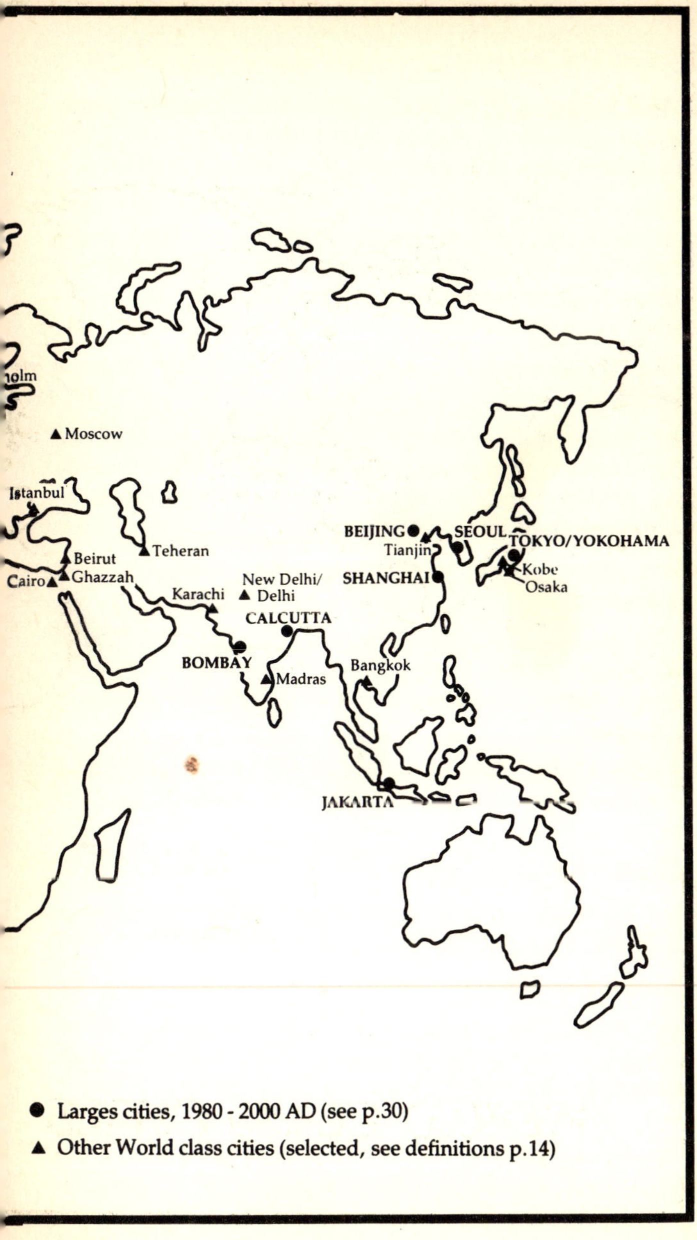

olm
Moscow
Istanbul
Teheran
Beirut
Cairo
Ghazzah
New Delhi/
Delhi
Karachi
BEIJING
Tianjin
SEOUL
TOKYO/YOKOHAMA
Kobe
Osaka
SHANGHAI
CALCUTTA
BOMBAY
Madras
Bangkok
JAKARTA
● Larges cities, 1980 - 2000 AD (see p.30)
▲ Other World class cities (selected, see definitions p.14)

Definitions

Church This includes all denominations, their local congregations, house churches and para-church agencies – any gathering of any sort of people who own the Lordship of Jesus.

Cities, urban regions, agglomerations These terms are used indiscriminately to refer to large urban areas. Usually the 'city' is the core of the 'urban region' or 'agglomeration'. Many urban regions are formed of scores of towns and cities converging.

First World The developed world of Europe, North America and Australasia.

Home and Foreign Mission Boards The main American denominations and some UK ones manage mission by these boards. In Britain, however, most foreign mission activities are managed by independent missionary societies.

Network A group of people who relate informally, without any constitution.

Primary relationship A relationship generated through family, neighbourhood, leisure or workplace, where people know each other's names and have recognition and friendship in varying degrees.

Primary cities Cities, mainly capital cities, which combine a number of functions: commercial, political, symbolic, etc. See p.38ff.

Second World The Communist bloc.

Secondary relationship Casual relationships with strangers – made in shops, on public transport, on the streets.

Turf The area controlled by a youth gang in an American city.

Two-thirds World The remaining areas of the world not included above – mostly the developing world but also including some highly developed Eastern and African countries.

World-class cities Cities of more than one million inhabitants, and of world significance. There are at least 290 cities of this size today, and Raymond Bakke regards 250 of these as having world significance.

1
From the Cowsheds to Chicago
A personal journey

A call to the city

I was born in 1938 in a remote rural valley near to the Canadian border in Washington State. It was 30 miles to the nearest town down a rough gravel road, and I sometimes missed a month of school each year because of the snow. I lived among the tall trees with ice-cream-cone mountains all around. The scattered homesteaders in the valley were all Norwegian Lutherans, mostly related to me.

My family were peasant stock who had emigrated from Norway. My mother refused to allow Norwegian to be spoken in our house, and did not want her sons growing up with 'accents'. This may have been because there was intense anti-German feeling in America at that time, and Norway was considered to be pro-Nazi, especially after Hitler had said that the Norwegians were good people. My father and mother wanted us to be wholly American, and discouraged any interest in the 'old country'. This was very common, and a whole generation of Americans from many countries suffered like us from being cut off from their pasts during the Second World War.

My brother Denny tells a story which illustrates our rural, insular origins. After completing a University degree, he won a scholarship for postgraduate study at Harvard. My father said, 'Denny, I don't think you should go to Harvard. I have never heard of it. I don't think it is a very good school. Besides, you are already a graduate of the University of Puget Sound!'.

Our family were loggers, and I cut trees and milked cows. I had lived in Alaska for a while but had never been south of

Seattle, and for many years had no ideas beyond logging or farming.

I attended a little one-room Lutheran church where we held a service in Norwegian with Communion for the older people. The minister was a layman, an itinerant carpenter. When I was about twelve, I was given my first job in the church: I became the librarian, with two shelves of books, and I took the job very seriously. After a few piano lessons I also became the Sunday School pianist. I came each Sunday with a few songs I could play, and I was in trouble if they chose something which was not on my list. My involvement with that little church gave me tremendous joy. Then the Scandinavian and other Lutheran churches merged to form the American Lutheran Church, and some remote bureaucrat decided to close our church down.

My Sunday School teacher taught our class of three for 10 years (one of the class members was my cousin, who is now a missionary in Zambia). That teacher poured his life into me. When Billy Graham or Youth for Christ teams came to Seattle – a hundred miles away – he would take us to hear them. I had never known a time when I was not a believer, but my commitment to serve the Lord with my life came one night when all three of us committed our lives together. How was I going to serve God? I had a vague idea that perhaps I would be a missionary.

I was 18 when I met a youth leader who suggested that I should train in youth and music ministry at Moody Bible Institute in Chicago. Perhaps I could teach in a school as a 'tent-maker', and be a youth leader and sports coach as well. I had not heard of Moody, but the plan did seem to offer some way out of our home valley.

Moody – into the city

So, in 1956, I travelled for three days and nights by Greyhound bus and was plunged into the middle of this amazing city – the biggest and most exciting city I could ever imagine. Chicago at that time had more people than 40 American states – and is still more populous than 25 of them, with nearly 7 million people. I hopped subways all over town to see its different sectors.

Moody Bible Institute was my bridge into the twentieth century. It was not really a very good urban training school: its staff did not live in the city, nor did they understand it, but the Institute was more open then than it became later. It seems to me that since the urban riots of the 1960s Moody has become more insulated from the city and involved in middle-class values.

Moody was nevertheless a good bridge for me. It did not confine us to the classroom, but threw us into all kinds of ministries to sink or swim. The city began to grow on me. I was sent to a big county hospital and told to witness to 50 black patients in one of the rooms. I had hardly ever seen a black person, let alone tried to witness to one. Then I was placed in a little Sunday School in the ghetto, then in a youth group in a black school. I was utterly bewildered and frustrated, but I was desperately interested in urban ministry, even though I had only the sketchiest idea of its implications.

Seattle – student and pastor

When I left Moody in 1959, I went on to study history and political science at Seattle Pacific College. Seattle then had about 600,000 people – about a million with its suburban region. This was useful to me, as it was a city small enough to be understood. It was an international port city and the company town of Boeing, the aerospace contractors.

In Seattle I lived with the Regional Director of Inter-Varsity Christian Fellowship, and met other students of all disciplines. For the first time, my faith was challenged by people who were working in nuclear physics, ethics, international relations or Russian studies. At our weekend Bible studies we had students from every subject and every country. I was forced to realise that my faith was largely inherited; forced to sort out faith from culture and to see what my personal faith and calling amounted to. The college offered a very heady and exotic environment.

By this time I was married. Corean is a musician, largely self-taught, with a rural southern background. She attended a one-room school in the Ozarks with all eight grades in one class. She strongly opposed the white southern racism, however, and at Moody she was distinguished by having a black room-mate, for whom she had specifically asked. Under her influence, and through reading *Stride Toward Freedom* by Martin Luther King, I was made aware of the racial ferment then developing in the United States.

During my college years I was an assistant pastor doing youth work at a church in Seattle. I was also Director of Choirs – I would do anything to put bread on the table! The church I joined was the Northern Baptist Church, and this was hard for my Lutheran family to accept. My grandparents felt that a Norwegian could not be a Christian unless he were a Lutheran, and I felt alienated from them for years. (Since then some of my family have become Pentecostals, so now our family gatherings are ecumenical in tone. We have learned to understand each other, and to share one another's values and faith. We sing the same songs, and teach our children to respect the diversity of the Body.)

After two years the pastor of my church left, and I found myself as interim pastor of an inner-city church with 300 members. During this period the Boeing works in the city closed, and I discovered how important his job is to urban man. It was difficult enough to minister to people who seemed to be mere extensions of the machines they worked on, doing dull repetitive work under pressure all day. But when the works closed, they were discarded by the company, just like disused machines themselves, and for many of them this amounted to loss of their identity. It produced immense personal problems, as well as social and financial ones. I realised that people were affected by their jobs and their environment, and so by political and business decisions made far away.

Thus, during my Seattle years, most of the main motivating themes of my ministry were established. What I had not yet done was to put it all together and function as an urban pastor. The final key was provided by a dry, dusty biography which changed my life. I am in urban ministry because of that book more than any other single thing.

Charles Simeon – urban pastor

The book was Moule's biography of Charles Simeon, published in 1895. Simeon had been a student of the theological faculty of King's College, Cambridge, in England. The famous university town was not as pretty in the late eighteenth century as it is now – in fact, it was a mess. Rural people were pouring from the impoverished countryside to fuel the Industrial Revolution. The well-to-do Cambridge residents and students hated these poor people who filled the crumbling hovels in the back streets of the city, and termed them 'riff-raff'.

Simeon walked through the city and stood outside the 700-year-old Holy Trinity Church, naively praying, 'Lord, give me this church so that I may minister to these people.' The church had been Catholic, then Anglican, and was now reduced to a tiny congregation, most of whom were quite indifferent to the plight of the masses outside the church. The bishop made Simeon the vicar because he had no one else interested in this unappealing situation.

Simeon began his ministry by going from door to door through his parish, approaching people with the words, 'My name is Simeon. I have called to enquire if I can do anything for your welfare.' His friendliness so affected the poor peasants that they began to attend the church. Unfortunately, their smelly clothes and unwashed state offended the better-off members who paid rents to the church for their pews. They were appalled by the company they were forced to keep and protested to the bishop to get rid of this man who was running their church. The bishop kept Simeon on, saying that a little life was better than death.

The paid-pew crowd had not finished yet. They locked their pews so they were not available in the mornings, and hired a guest lecturer to preach to them on Sunday afternoons, in the manner to which they were accustomed. Undaunted, Simeon bought timber out of his £49-a-year salary, and made portable benches for his Sunday-morning congregation. Every week he would set them in the aisles and foyer, then open the doors and invite the poor of the city to enter.

This went on for 11 years, and Simeon's patience was sustained by a philosophy that 'If half the people get a double blessing, I'll be satisfied.' In Simeon's twelfth year revival came, the wall of conflict came down, and the congregation united. Simeon stayed there for a further 54 years and his career was astonishing. He continued to work with the poor. He was five times Dean of the theological faculty at King's College, and influenced and informed dozens of young pastors. Like Luther, he never stopped lecturing.

Out of the ministry he founded came Inter-Varsity, the Cambridge Seven, a mission to China, and C T Studd and Henry Martyn, who went to India and translated the Bible into Urdu. Simeon created a network of influence throughout England as his young pastors began to find their way into all its industrial cities.

Each month he travelled to London to meet William Wilberforce, Lord Shaftesbury, members of Parliament and others in the Clapham Sect. They had one agenda: to abolish slavery in the British Empire. As I read of them, I began to feel a kindred spirit with all these people who had been concerned with urban mission issues more than 100 years ago.

When Britain colonised Australia with convicts, it was Simeon who appointed a chaplain to accompany the first boatload to Sydney. This chaplain created the Archdiocese of Sydney, and Simeon's mark is still on the Anglican church in that city.

As I read Moule's biography, I knew my life was being changed. Here was a pastor with an urban vision who worked with the poor, who was an evangelist, who discipled people, lectured at the university, wrote magnificent commentaries and still had time to go to London and work to stop the slave trade. I had a vision of what urban pastors and churches could do. The relationships of evangelistic, social, academic ministries, with pastoral caring and political activity, all came together in the career of Charles Simeon. He related the local church to its city, its country and to foreign mission.

I made Simeon my model. I decided to return to my studies

and prepare myself to emulate what he had done. I returned to Chicago in 1965.

Community and church

In 1965 we lost a daughter at birth: Corean had contracted German measles when we were staying with a friend. We buried our daughter back home in our small rural community among my whole family. This was a real Ebenezer experience ('Thus far has the Lord helped us' I Sam 7:12). We left our little child and travelled to Chicago with our sons, then aged two and four.

My postgraduate studies in theology, Hebrew and Greek were at Trinity Evangelical Divinity School and McCormick Theological Seminary, and I was commuting 25 miles to get there. Following Charles Simeon, I knew I had to live in the inner city, so Corean and I and our two small boys had moved into a one-mile-square block in Chicago's South Side.

There were further trials ahead. I blew up our building, breaking 45 windows, by lighting a faulty stove which was leaking gas. The explosion lifted the ceiling and blew out walls in the neighbouring buildings – and I survived! I went to hospital, badly burned, with my eyes nearly closed. During my first year trying to be like Charles Simeon I found myself with my skin hanging off like moss, fed intravenously, and receiving skin grafts.

My wife fell down the stairs and broke her foot – and we were broke, too. Around us the city was rioting and our area was turfed by warring gangs. This was a tough, high stress year, but the Lord was refining me and teaching me a great deal. I knew that good can come from all discipline, if you are open to it. I had never suffered in my life until then, and I began to look at myself, the city and the church in a different way.

The city seemed to be blowing up. Our local secondary school had 2,300 pupils of 54 nationalities, being taught in 11 languages. Race riots raged throughout the 1960s and peaked after the murder of Martin Luther King in 1968. Around 32 gangs turfed our community, and I buried kids who were killed with guns just because they entered enemy gang territory. Some of the windows of the church were shot out by a drunken Mexican just after a Sunday service. Arson was prevalent; during the worst year 1,300 fires in the parish left 27 of our church families homeless. Even the schools were turfed and the children needed gang permission to use a certain staircase or attend a certain class. Armed policemen patrolled the school hall, corridors and toilets.

Today, little has changed. More than half our community is foreign born – about 2.3% Asian, 14% Spanish and a variety of others. A further 39% of the population are American blacks, many of them from the southern states. In my community we have the victims of violence in South-east Asia, of black racism, and of Hispanic oppression. There are refugees from Iraq and Beirut, and others shattered by their experiences of war and other exploitation. This environment shapes my perspective on the family in the urban community.

The community overcrowds its buildings. Garbage piles up and rats flourish. Children are poisoned by lead from crumbling pre-war paintwork and pipes. Half our households have single-parent female heads. Whole generations grow up without seeing anyone go out to work.

The Vietnam War was disastrous – politically, for America, and socially, for our cities. Most of the healthy kids were drafted, and the community was affected. All the kids with police records were left behind and gang warfare multiplied. We were ravaged by delinquency.

During my seminary period I began to pastor Fairfield Avenue Baptist Church. The core of the congregation was 11 adult members, the youngest of whom was 54. I was its first full-time pastor. My plan was to take this church for a year while I completed my studies at Trinity and McCormick. I then planned to do a doctorate at Yale, studying the early Greek cities. I never got there, and I stayed with this church for 10 years.

In 1965 I met radical clergy for the first time. One liberal theologian argued that conservative evangelicals could not survive in the city. To take the Bible literally is to become anti-urban. God's favourite people were shepherds; his next favourite people were vine-growers and farmers; and his least favourite people were urban dwellers. This argument was important to me. If indeed God's agenda were to empty the city and destroy it, I would not want to resist, but it was a concept I could not accept. We suffered in those early years, but I did not feel that God was driving us from the city; rather that we were being taught and refined by sharing in the city's pain.

I was equally disillusioned by the churches. Captive to their class and culture, they were unable to minister to the poor and multiracial urban communities. I had committed my life to service in the Church, and now I found the Church irrelevant.

In this state of confusion I looked about me at the city I had chosen for my ministry. What I found was a place with its own peculiar history and development, but which now is typical of cities all over the world in its political, racial and religious problems.

Understanding Chicago

If you were coming to Chicago from San Francisco or Washington DC the city would seem old, dirty and noisy. It is a surprise to discover that it is fairly new – founded in 1834 and incorporated in 1837. It has always looked old, because this industrial city, located where lake and river met the railroads, was built by people from the old countries of Europe, and they built Chicago generally like the places they had left.

Between 1834 and 1860 the emerging Chicago was bustling, raucous and muddy. The name means 'bad smell' in the local Indian language. During the American Civil War of 1861-5 it became the headquarters in the West for the encirclement of the Confederacy.

Then came 50 years of massive growth, with railroads spreading out across the prairie states into the west, making Chicago the greatest animal slaughtering and grain centre in the world. To the north was the iron-ore of Minnesota and Wisconsin; to the south the giant coalfields of the Appalachians. Chicago became the centre of a gigantic iron and steel industry. This was European Chicago. The Irish came originally to dig the canals, but quickly captured the urban trinity of policeman, priest and politician – politics, law and religion being old hobbies of theirs in their troubles with the English. Huge numbers of Germans, Poles, Italians and many others arrived. This was the era that built the city and shaped its institutions.

In the late 1930s the country's population moved northwards to fuel the war machine and to escape the ravages of the Depression and racism. The southerners found Chicago a 'foreign' city, run mainly by those European immigrants, who by now had moved to the suburbs. After the Second World War the deep coal-mines closed as natural gas and oil from Texas and Oklahoma became available, and the workforce from the mines also came seeking work in industrial Chicago.

Since 1970 Chicago has been internationalising again, with a rapidly growing Hispanic population – mainly from Mexico and Puerto Rico – and very large numbers from the Middle East and Asia. There is a growing Muslim population, with 34 mosques in the city.

Politics in Chicago

Chicago is controlled by the Democratic Party machine – its County Chairman decides on the candidates and nominees for offices. Everything in Chicago is political, from the garbage (which is only collected in certain areas depending on who won the latest election) to the Building Inspectors (who may be pressured into closing buildings owned by opposition supporters).

Until recently, it was also controlled by a whites-only system. However, in a recent election, Harold Washington took on this racist and political battle and was elected as the first black mayor. This has been seen as a tremendous achievement by a coalition of churches who worked together to give him support. His election has produced changes which the multiracial community hardly dreamed of before.

In positions of authority, Washington has achieved a racial balance, as blacks and Hispanics with Harvard degrees are appointed, as well as well-qualified whites, as directors of housing, police, health and community services. O'Hare airport employs 35,000 people; at one time, the only black business involved was the men's room shoe-shine. However, in a recent extension, 20 of the 50 business concessions went to minority groups.

There have been major political changes in the last 30 years all over America. Blacks are now politically visible in the power structure, with 5,000 black and Hispanic elected offices. This is, however, only 1% of all the elected offices in the USA. The black population alone is 12%. So the blacks have made a gain from nothing to 1% in 30 years. However, many of the gains are being made in areas from which power is departing – it is a hollow victory to end up being mayor of a city with no resources for schools, civic services, police and so on. We celebrate on the one hand the emergence of minorities into political office, but on the other hand a new paternalism is arising. These mayors have to go begging for resources to white legislatures on behalf of their populations. It is a new kind of humiliation.

However, I am hopeful that a competent urban leadership is emerging. It is encouraging to turn on the TV and see articulate blacks as well as whites speaking from a position of authority.

One last word must concern the Mafia – partly because everyone associates Chicago with this, and partly because theirs is a para-legal power which infiltrated politics.

Chicago between the wars had a vast Catholic population divided mainly between the Irish, Italians and Sicilians. The Irish had captured the political machine, and the Italians and Sicilians created their own power structures in gangs. The Italians brought their village-gang structures into Chicago, based around very powerful and loyal extended families. The Mafia grew to immense proportions and took over the entire political machinery in the 1920s. The Protestant establishment in the East hated Catholicism, and the Prohibition Act of 1919 may be regarded by some as anti-Catholic legislation. It led to immense fortunes being made by the Mafia gangs.

The Mafia is no longer significant in big-city politics and

has moved into finance and entertainments, and runs the world-wide narcotics conspiracy centred on Miami. The Mafia is still mainly Italian and Sicilian and cannot work in multi-ethnic cities.

Multiracial Chicago

Chicago has always been multiracial – first the Europeans came, and now people from 60 or more countries have been added to its population. The southern blacks are another special group, and they too are divided. There are coal-culture, cotton-culture and tobacco-culture blacks, as well as subtle groupings based on gradation in skin colour. In five churches in a block on the South Side, the congregations could be graded by colour from light black to dark black. All five churches originated in Alabama.

Chicago was always two cities. Lake Front was WASP – wealthy, alienated, separated and protected; on the river were PIGS – Poles, Italians, Greeks and Slovacs. All these ethnic groupings are in constant change. We have different Spanish groups, American Indians, Iraqis and others from the Middle East. One day a group of little kids pushed me up against the wall and said, 'Mister, you're our hostage.' I looked at them and laughed and thought, what else would kids from the Middle East play during the great hostage crisis in Iran?

The churches are equally multiracial. In 1980, Chicago had 2,167 identifiable churches. Over 1,100 were black churches, and these were mostly located in 10 of the city's 77 neighbourhoods. I counted over 80 churches within a mile of my own building, and most of them used languages other than English.

The Roman Catholic Church has been faithful to Chicago in a way that the Protestants have not. The white Catholics fled to the suburbs with their Protestant neighbours, but the buildings and the priests stayed. The Church is now seeing a renaissance and has done a great deal to welcome the different groups of people. The fastest-growing church in Chicago in the 1970s was Holy Angels – a black Catholic church in the ghetto. Its different chapels are decorated in the styles of particular ethnic groups; it also has a Baptist chapel and one dedicated to Martin Luther King. The late Archbishop Cody was reputed to have disapproved, but the priest, Father Clements, is said to have told him, 'You can take it down if you like, but I can't guarantee your safety!' There are six Sunday services with six different styles of music. One service is a Rock Mass, and the sermon is delivered in ordinary language from the aisle, with crowds of kids sitting everywhere.

In the church of Corpus Christi, the 'afro' colours – black, green and red stripes – have been painted round the top of an otherwise very European, mediaeval-style sanctuary.

The Catholic Church combines a symbol of transcendence – the Mass – with a symbol of immanence – the Pope. It makes concessions to the city, with churches open all day for individual prayer and confession as well as for group life, with multiple masses through the day. Evangelicals generally have not made these concessions and have much to learn from Catholic practice.

Studying the city

This, then, was the particular environment in which I found myself in 1965. Poverty, social problems, political corruption, religious and racial divisions surrounded me, yet I knew that Chicago was not unique. All over the world the pattern seemed to be repeating itself, as the great cities grew ever larger and people moved in ever increasing numbers, not just from the countryside to the town, but from continent to continent. Cities were becoming more complex, multiracial and multifaith communities.

However, it seemed to me that if the problems were the same in many countries, some of the solutions should be common, too. So in my search for understanding of my own environment, I set myself the task of studying the city, to see what God is doing in this generation.

2
The Lord Is Shaking Up the World
A review of world population and urbanisation

When I began to look seriously at the problems of cities, I realised that the Lord is doing something very unusual in this generation. He seems to be shaking up the world. 'Go and make disciples of all nations.' Now we know where all the nations are – in the big cities. God has brought all the nations here – to wherever your big city is.

The historical background

Of course, there were substantial cities as early as biblical times. Nineveh is described in Jonah 4:11 (seventh century BC) as having 120,000 people. The ancient empires of the Middle East, described in the Bible, centred upon capital or primary cities – Assyria upon Nineveh, Babylonia upon Babylon, Israel upon Jerusalem.

Throughout the later Greek and Roman Empires the Mediterranean developed as the focus of the urban world, and by the time of Paul (AD 60), Rome housed about one million people. This area continued to be of primary importance throughout the next 13 centuries.

During the thirteenth and fourteenth centuries urban supremacy moved to Northern Europe. The Hanse ports of the Baltic, then Amsterdam and London looked to a growing Atlantic trade. The Italian States and Spain declined steadily as world powers, while France, Great Britain and the German States developed industrially and as global empires.

The Industrial Revolution of the late eighteenth century onwards occurred in the coal and iron fields of Europe, Britain and the United States, and this developed the ports which serviced their gigantic world-wide trade. Capital cities of these countries continued to dominate their urban growth with numerous financial services and manufacturing industries. Cities of several million people developed rapidly at this time: Berlin, Paris, London, New York and Chicago.

However, just as the Atlantic replaced the Mediterranean as the focus of world urbanisation between the fourteenth and early twentieth centuries, so has the Pacific rim of Asia now become the urban focus of the world – from Tokyo-Yokohama to Singapore. These urban areas front the massive populations of China and Japan and have emerged into economic and financial dominance. The Two-thirds World cities of Latin America, Africa and the Indian subcontinent are growing equally fast, but are characterised by extreme poverty. In December 1986 there were at least 290 cities of more than one million people. (This figure was calculated in a study by Dr David D Barrett in 1986.)

In the next seven seconds 31 babies will be born. Half of these babies will end up living in cities. This century has seen the most dramatic rise ever in world population, and growth will continue until around the year 2100, according to the United Nations. It should be noted that the rate of increase is slowing down.

Year	World Population (Millions)	Annual Rate % change
1925	2,000	
		1.5
1985	4,841	
		0.7
2100	10,200	

Most of the increase has taken place in the poorer regions of the world. Although the rate of increase is drastically slowing down, by the time births are no more than replacing deaths, the world population will be more than double its present figure.

Cities in the developed world

In both the USA and Europe, those cities which developed as a result of the Industrial Revolution grew fastest during the

The World's 10 Largest Agglomerations

(Showing population in millions)

1980		1985		1990 (predicted)		2000 (predicted)	
1. Tokyo/Yokohama	20.0	Tokyo/Yokohama	21.8	Tokyo/Yokohama	23.0	Mexico City	27.6
2. New York/NJ	17.7	Mexico City	18.4	Mexico City	21.8	Sao Paulo	26.0
3. Mexico City	15.1	New York/NJ	18.3	Shanghai	20.1	Tokyo/Yokohama	24.0
	15.0	Shanghai	17.5	New York/NJ	18.8	New York Area	23.0
5. Sao Paulo	12.6	Sao Paulo	15.0	Sao Paulo	17.5	Shanghai	23.0
6. Beijing	12.0	Beijing	14.0	Beijing	17.4	Beijing	20.0
7. Los Angeles/Long Beach	10.1	Los Angeles/Long Beach	10.9	Greater Bombay	11.8	Rio de Janeiro	19.0
8. Greater Buenos Aires	10.1	Greater Buenos Aires	10.8	Rio de Janeiro	11.7	Greater Bombay	17.0
9. Greater London	10.0	Rio de Janeiro	10.4	Calcutta	11.7	Calcutta	17.0
10. Paris	9.7	Seoul	10.2	Seoul	11.6	Jakarta	17.0

Source: *Estimates and Projections of Urban, Rural and City Populations, 1950-2025*, p.61, Table 8 (United Nations, 1982). (See also David Barrett's *World Christian Encyclopedia* for details.)

nineteenth century. Their population peaked in the early decades of the twentieth century, and they are now declining in numbers.

The three centuries of American history clearly illustrate the changes. In the first century people moved west, looking for farmland. In the second century they went to the north and east into the industrial and commercial cities. This century has seen a shift of power to the 'southern crescent' stretching from Carolina to Florida along the flourishing south. Florida, Texas and California are the fastest-growing states. In this third great shift of population and prosperity the old cities of the north and east have been left behind in decline.

The spread of urban culture

However, this does not mean that we are becoming less urbanised; rather that urban culture is spreading out and colonising the suburbs, small towns and rural areas. The city is less of a place and more of a process, taking its franchised outlets to the small towns, and its standard newspapers and television broadcasts to the remotest rural village.

The governments of many Western countries have encouraged the dispersal of population and industries. In Britain enormous New Towns and 'overspill' programmes were carried out in the three decades after the Second World War. In the United States the Mortgage Act and the Highway Development Act of 1947 led to the massive freeway and motorway systems, and a government-subsidised exodus from the cities to the suburbs and beyond. These financial and highway provisions enable people to live long distances from their work, and reward them for doing so. Large companies move to new, larger premises in the suburbs, along good road routes so that employees can live still further out. Tax concessions are given more often for new buildings than for renewal of buildings in old communities. A prosperous family moving to its Garden of Eden sees its move as an individual issue, but the policies which made the move possible are anti-community, creating suburbs and tearing up communities in the cities.

Via the media, urban culture reaches into every home, however remote. For example, when Johnny Carson uses Los Angeles as a TV stage prop for his nightly excursions into rural and small-town America, he urbanises formerly rural space. Television exports urban persons, values and products that create new social awareness. One might see every TV personality as an urban cultural John the Baptist, crying, 'The city is coming! The city is coming!' This universal awareness of city life is a psychological urban sprawl more rapid and engulfing than any developing suburb.

It is realistic, then, to see the decentralisation of American and European cities throughout their entire cultures not as a decline in urbanisation, but profoundly the opposite. The same forces that produced Chicago, Detroit and Miami have gone everywhere. There is no escape from urbanisation as a process. The exodus of families and workforces results in suburban sprawl and the growth of small towns and villages; this represents the extension of cities and not the escape from them that many frightened and 'flightful' people have assumed.

The century of homeless man

As the developed cities spread, their centres still act as magnets for the poor and dispossessed. Thus even an English city like Liverpool, which has seen its population decline by half to less than 500,000, still has a substantial ethnic minority including 10,000 Chinese.

There are 223 nations in the world, and in my one-mile-square block in the middle of Chicago, 60 of those nations (27%) are represented. In May 1982 the *New York Times* survey of Chinatown found refugees from every province of mainland China – in four blocks in the middle of New York City.

The United States is a country of immigrants. During the nineteenth century they poured in in waves to escape poverty, famine or persecution. 'Give me your tired, your poor, your huddled masses yearning to be free . . . send those homeless, tempest-tossed to me' says the inscription on the Statue of Liberty. It still goes on. In the decade of the 1970s the number of immigrants into the USA equalled the 8.8 million of 1900-1910. Since the Second World War, the racial composition of big cities has been drastically altered by internal migrations within the USA, of blacks from the southern states to the northern cities.

Whereas previous migration was by sea from Europe, mainly to New York, the 'southern crescent' is now the immigration zone. Miami is de facto the capital of Latin America, and at least one million Hispanics pour illegally over the 2,400-mile border between Mexico and the United States every year. With four and a half million Hispanics, Los Angeles is now the second-largest 'Mexican' city, while Houston is the fastest-growing one. Four-fifths of all Houston's schoolchildren are either Hispanic, black or Asian. The southern American cities are seeing a huge concentration of the poor, and Two-thirds World characteristics coexist uneasily with affluent American communities.

Refugees

Refugees are an age-old problem, but modern methods of transport have made possible international movement on a scale hitherto unknown. The Second World War displaced 40 million people from their homes in Europe alone, but 83% of these stayed within their national boundaries. Nowadays international displacement is common. About half of today's refugees are Africans moving from one country to another. 'The extent and urgency of these situations is unprecedented' according to Ninan Koshy of the World Council of Churches.

Almost all the countries in Western Europe have received their share of this refugee movement. Most former colonial powers have become hosts to people from the former colonies, much to the consternation of the natives (what might be described as 'the Empires striking back'). Urban riots have occurred all over the globe, in which the presence of urban migrants and refugees, and reactions to them, have played a role. London was the head of the world – now the world is in London. In Amsterdam certain communities have 16% of their population from Goa, Molucca and Surinam, while in Paris there are 300,000 Algerians. Other immigrant groups are the half-million Finns in Sweden, 50,000 Yugoslavs in Stockholm, and Turks in most of the cities of West Germany.

Urban interdependence

Refugees are those people forced to move by war, famine or persecution: migrants move 'freely' to find better work or conditions. However, it is governments and multinational companies who drive whole communities to poverty, and so the distinction between 'free' and 'forced' movements is not a clear one. A city may appear to have economic independence, but it must always be seen to be part of the larger national system, influenced by political decisions and financial opportunism.

In the first year of the Reagan administration $40 billion was removed from social budgets (at that time mostly spent in the northern and eastern cities) and added to the Pentagon military budget (which is mostly spent in the growth areas of the south). Federal decisions of this magnitude, made in Washington, affect dozens of cities and millions of people, and decide which urban regions flourish or decline.

When I began ministry in Seattle in 1959, it was the Boeing town. Almost the entire economy depended on that company. In 1961 the huge contract for the TFX aeroplane (which had already been given to Boeing) was diverted to General Dynamics in Texas. The deal was a political one worked out by Lyndon Johnson when he became Vice-President to Kennedy. John Kennedy was a Roman Catholic: he had picked Johnson because he brought with him the support of many Protestant voters from the south. Johnson was rewarded by the shift of many military and industrial contracts from the north to the south.

The economy of an entire town, and the incomes of thousands of families, were changed almost overnight by decisions taken 3,000 miles away. I began to see that a decision made in Washington to move resources to Texas affected us in Seattle; that cities are not just sets of people but systems like those of the body, part of a larger whole. Cities must be seen as systems themselves which also operate within national and international systems.

Urban growth in the Two-thirds World

We have seen that the fastest-growing cities today are those in the Two-thirds World. But their experiences of urbanisation are very different from those of the developed world, which passed through a parallel phase in the nineteenth century.

Firstly, the scale is enormous, compared with earlier growth. Manchester was a wonder of the world in the early nineteenth century, and people came from every country to view with awe and horror the amazing and dreadful things happening there. Manchester grew from 70,000 in 1801 to 243,000 in 1841, and increased steadily to its peak of about 800,000 by the First World War. Today, Mexico City grows by half a million people a year, and Bangkok by 750,000 a year. These cities add more people annually than Manchester totalled after two centuries of industrial growth.

Modern urbanisation combines large-scale immigration from rural areas, with exploding birth rates. These Two-thirds World cities have very young populations with no history and without the constraints found in rural communities. They are rootless, mobile, media-tuned, volatile, and demand that the quality of life will improve. The peak of urban violence, which has probably passed in Western cities, has yet to come in these flashpoint human aggregations.

A second difference is the prospects for employment. The old cities had a wealth of capital and developed labour-intensive industries. Now, even in Two-thirds World cities, where labour is plentiful and cheap, capital-intensive economies are developing, and high-technology industries are gradually reducing the amount of manpower necessary. At the moment jobs are still growing in those cities, but as these countries strive to catch up with the developed world, the prospect for the future is bleak.

The Two-thirds World cities are running against the limits of their environments – oil, raw materials, even air. Jakarta is now the world's largest city without a sewage system. Its eight and a half million people live in a huge garbage-dump. If they burn the garbage, it poisons the air; if they bury it, it poisons the water. In most of the Two-thirds World cities there are whole industries living in the garbage – sorting it, selling it and thus recycling it.

However desperate Liverpool, Chicago or Pittsburgh may seem, there is a vast difference in degree between them and the cities of the developing countries.

Family life

In Africa men are moving into the cities, leaving their wives, children and parents on the tribal land. The men move into the cities on their own, and prostitution moves in with them. Family and community breakdown on a large scale occurs in African cities. Roughly a quarter of the working-age population of all African cities is unemployed and a further quarter is 'under-employed', in part-time, low-value jobs. This is a social time-bomb more powerful than abject poverty, for people who have rapidly rising and unmet expectations.

In Latin America conditions are quite different. The whole family moves to the city together including grandmother, the goat, and all the family possessions. They set up home in a *barrio* or district: of all Latin Americans, 64% now live in cities.

When a young couple moves from a village to the city, the unskilled husband works perhaps on a building site. His wife dresses smartly to work on computers in a down-town office block. He expects her to behave like a village wife, but she has become bicultural – village wife and independent urban woman. The city threatens their family life and tears it apart.

Women aged 15-19 are the largest group moving into the Latin American cities, in contrast to the African situation noted above. They become liberated and form the growing professional groups of those cities. Very quickly they begin to demand other rights and privileges, and challenge traditional rural marriage values. These cities recruit and then transform these human resources.

Many urban women trade sex for security from their men. Some poor women deliberately make themselves fat and unattractive so that their drunken husbands will not want sex with them. I have been told, 'If I look attractive, I'm going to get beaten up by all kinds of men, including my own husband.'

There are political pressures on nuclear families. A large backlog of Bangladeshi women are still waiting to join their men in Britain. In South Africa men are compelled to live in dormitories around the mining towns, with their wives on tribal homelands perhaps hundreds of miles away. The North American cities have concentrations of migrants from all over Latin America and elsewhere. It is common for these to form new families; some maintain links with the families they have abandoned back home.

Massive migration, poor housing and unemployment all add up to vast pressures on family life, which is fragmented and debased.

Classifying world cities

Early urbanologists classified cities by place and form, but later ones, led by Louis Mumford, defined them by functions – the rôles they play in the larger society. There is one aspect of the form of cities which Mumford regards as unique. Cities contain and transmit cultures; by bringing together all the separate parts (as racial groups find themselves living side by side) they enable direct relationships that become engines and catalysts of cultural change.

It will be helpful to urban Christians, and to the developing argument of this book, to outline a few of the possible classifications by function.

Cultural cities lead the culture in fashions, trends and ideas. Paris, Oxford, Boston and San Francisco include this cultural rôle among their functions.

Political and administrative cities contain governments and their bureaucracies. Their product is power and decisions. Examples are Washington DC, New Delhi and Brasilia.

Other cities are primarily *industrial*. A third of the entire economic product of India passes through Bombay. Sao Paulo (with about 15 million people), Chicago-Gary and

Bombay function like engines and throb with power. They are dirty, ugly, noisy, blue-collar factory cities. They have more in common with each other than with the other types of city.

Commercial cities function like giant markets. New York is like a huge bazaar. The purpose of these cities is to make money, and their appearance often indicates the presence of wealth.

Some cities are *symbolic*. Soweto, Belfast, Berlin, Beirut or Jerusalem symbolise the divisions within their countries, oppression, warfare or religious hatred.

The cities which combine all these rôles are called *primary cities:* London, Paris, or the capitals of most Two-thirds World countries.

Some primary cities

Bangkok

Bangkok, Thailand, is a typical primary city. It has six million people in more than a thousand slum areas, and adds about 750,000 people annually to its population. The slums act as little entrepreneurial pockets of cheap labour, drawing people from the poor rural areas. Women and children sew up shirts for 10 cents each. The shirts are sold in Oxford Street, London, with enormous profits for all the middlemen. The cheap labour undercuts British wages and bypasses 150 years of British industrial legislation.

Bangkok's economy illustrates the power of multinational economy. In 1978 the international economy exceeded for the first time the total of the world's national economies. The multinational companies control the destiny and welfare of whole countries, and are part of the process whereby primary cities sprawl and dominate their countries. The companies have their headquarters and factories in these cities where they can control production and draw upon a huge labour force for the lowest wages. The city then has to find all the other costs of these workers – housing, education, hospitals and transport. These cities become giant parasites upon the rest of their countries, absorbing disparate shares of investment capital. The rural areas become even more run down, and so the incentives to move to the primary cities are increased even more.

Governments, on the whole, are inordinately proud of these cities. Political leaders rush into the twentieth century with showcase international airports and prestige hotels, absorbing yet more capital which might have been spent on rural infrastructures to improve conditions outside the city. They exploit resources, both financial and human, which could be used to create a more just distribution of wealth and amenities, and concentrate them in the capital cities. Is it any wonder that the poor go on flocking hopefully towards the bright lights of the city?

Mexico City

This is now the second largest city in the world, with 18 million people. By 1995 it is expected – if present trends continue – to have 25 million people, and by 2000, at least 27.6 million people. It contains a quarter of the country's population and grows by a million people a year – 600,000 by births and 400,000 by migration from the rural parts of Mexico.

The median age of Mexico City is 14.2, compared with the 31 of Chicago. This means that half of the population of Mexico City is aged 14.2 or under; and half that of Chicago is aged under 31. The city is a gigantic orphanage with 9 million babies and children. There is not a city in the Two-thirds World – as far as I know – with a median age over 20.

Mexico City needs one million new jobs a year to absorb the young people entering the labour market. The best-ever figure for new jobs was 400,000 in 1978 at the peak of the oil boom.

The vast agglomeration is at an altitude of 7,500 feet and has only half the oxygen of a city at sea level. It is surrounded by mountains so that industrial fumes are trapped. Breathing its air is equivalent to smoking several packets of cigarettes a day. The increased toxicity of the inhabitants' blood and their increased rate of heartbeat are measurable. Pollution, lead and carbon monoxide are poisoning the inhabitants and possibly changing their behaviour.

Mexico City is a fearsome parable of the urban explosion engulfing the Two-thirds World. The Presidents of Mexico, elected for seven-year terms, make their mark on this capital city. They have consistently invested nearly all their resources and industries there. The city is a gigantic magnet, but it is out of control, stealing air, water, people and every resource from the nation.

London

Greater London and the Home Counties had 10 million people in 1985 (according to the UK government estimate), one-fifth of the population of England and Wales. Its inner areas were declining, but the population of the greater urban area had spread out, with growth in the suburban and rural belts. The population of Islington – an inner borough – declined from 410,000 people in 1939 to 61,000 people in 1981. In 1939 the population was almost entirely English; by 1981 it included, according to some estimates, as many as 50,000 Cypriots and 15,000 Irish, with large numbers of West Indians and Asians.

Similarly, the population of Tower Hamlets borough declined from 600,000 in 1900 to 142,000 in 1981. This borough has always hosted refugees, from the Huguenots in the eighteenth century to the Jews in the early twentieth century, and now Bangladeshis and other Asians.

Throughout inner London and the other old urban areas of Britain there has been a breakdown of the traditional extended family structure. British planning between 1950 and 1975 demolished large areas of inner-city housing condemned as slums, and built large overspill estates. Usually the younger families moved to these, leaving behind their middle-aged or elderly parents. In East London about one-third of all households consist of single people, and most of these are elderly. Extended family structures seem unlikely to re-form or survive in the British cities.

London is now one of the most multi-ethnic cities in Europe, with a growing Muslim population, and large Afro-Caribbean, Cypriot, Greek, Italian, Chinese and other communities. Its characteristics are mirrored by the other main urban areas of Britain which, between 1951 and 1975, lost 30% of their population and 20% of their employment. Their surrounding rural areas and small towns have gained population and jobs. The prosperous middle classes commute through the declining inner areas to the city centres, which still look and feel prosperous. Those manual workers still employed travel to scattered industrial estates on the outskirts.

In Clydeside, commuting increased by 350% between 1951 and 1971; while in Liverpool 88% of the city's jobs were done by its own residents in 1951, but only 58% in 1976. Between 1970 and 1984, Liverpool lost 140,000 jobs. The professional and manual workers now pass each other going in opposite directions on their way to work. In 1951 the cities had 40% of Britain's workforce. This figure was reduced to 24% by 1971 and will be lower now.

Even when there is increased employment available in a locality, it does not follow that the local people get the jobs, as they may well be unqualified. In London in 1985 there were only 19 vacancies for every 500 unskilled people unemployed. There is tremendous diversity within the cities. In 1985 inner-city Hackney had an unemployment rate of 24%, while the rate in prosperous suburban Sutton was only 5%. People under 20, over 50, or not white, were more likely to be unemployed.

Effects of city life

The effects of city life vary according to the type of city, its history, the part of it that the individual occupies, and his income and social background. Most striking are those features of poor communities which must influence our evangelism and which the Christian family must understand if it is to survive city life.

Some years ago a young woman – Kitty Genovese – was relentlessly stabbed to death in New York while more than 20 people heard her screams and watched her die. They chose not to get involved nor even to report the crime. It took about 20 minutes for her assailant to kill her, and as she screamed and ran back and forth across the street people sat and watched from their apartment windows.

This episode thoroughly shocked Americans, and studies were launched into this urban indifference to the plight of a neighbour. How can people stand around and watch someone get killed and not get involved?

The massive study found that urban people suffer from 'psychological overload'. To prevent 'overload' we have filters which enable us to cope with noise, the constant bombardment of sales messages and thousands of casual daily relationships. People survive in the city by wearing mental blinkers: by filtering what they accept, and by opting out of relationships and situations. People survive in the city by not having to think about what they do. Sometimes we are startled and think, 'I wonder whether I drove through that red light?' Our reactions have become unconscious.

What do you suppose, then, is the effect of door-to-door calling upon strangers? Very low. People live in locked buildings because they do not want any more casual relationships. They can only handle so many, and in a city – where all aspects of reality are intensified – they refuse to communicate, in order to survive.

People have three networks of 'primary' relationships:

1. Biological – family and extended family, which may be local or distant.
2. Geographical – people we know because of where we live.
3. Vocational – the people with whom we work.

In rural areas people gain identities through the first two networks: their parents and where they live identify them. In a small town we know everybody. We have a primary relationship even to the town drunk. We know all the political leaders, the elders and the children. They all know us – where we live, our parents, sisters and brothers.

When we move to the city we are identified by our jobs,

and nearly all our relationships are 'secondary' or casual. Amidst this kaleidoscopic and bewildering environment we get lost – 'when the tide goes out, each shrimp has its own puddle'.

Now let me share an experiment which my students do. Go to any busy street in your town and ask the men and women walking briskly to work, 'Who are you?' I predict that most of them will tell you not who they are but what they do. 'Who are you, madam?' – 'I am a secretary.' 'Who are you, sir?' – 'I'm a lawyer.' 'Who are you, sir?' – 'Well, I work in that building over there. I'm a clerk.'

It is for this reason that unemployment is not just an economic crisis, but one of identity. Urban people are insecure, and if they lose their jobs, they suffer more severely than those in rural areas. My father lived through the Depression and had a succession of jobs and spells of unemployment, yet for all this he has not experienced a crisis of identity. He is a rural person, living where he grew up and secure in his family. His family is organised around the cemetery and the church – half his family is in the former and the other half in the latter – a secure world.

In cities unemployment is altogether different, and we are ineffective in Christian ministry to the unemployed because we do not understand what unemployment does. When the Boeing company in Seattle lost the big aeroplane contract, it threw away its workforce like garbage. People lost not only their jobs but their identity. They looked inward, blamed themselves and began to feel unimportant. They lived on the margins of society, looking on. Many of them were driven to alcoholism, sexual abandonment, lack of integrity and hedonism of all kinds. Unemployment is a world-wide urban crisis.

Urban people want, and hunger for, fellowship which is high quality and lasting. Neighbourhood taverns function as the therapy and fellowship centres night after night for many people. If you study these, you will find that drinking is incidental to the real purpose of the gathering. When Ralph Neighbour studied taverns in Houston, Texas, he concluded that people came looking for fellowship and a shoulder to cry on. Urban people protect themselves from casual and superficial relationships, because urban life is socially mobile with many people passing in and out of their lives. At the same time this testifies that they need a few continuing relationships in all kinds of congregational settings.

To the Christian, the answer to that need is obvious. Jesus Christ offers love and acceptance, the ultimate personal relationship, freely to all. The Christian community, working and worshipping together, offers fellowship and support. The Church has solutions to the most profound urban problems – so why is it not getting its message across? Why is it seen so often as out of date, out of touch and irrelevant?

I had studied the nature of cities, both in the developed world and in the Two-thirds World. I had seen how they are growing, how they function, and what effect city life has on people. So the next question to which I addressed myself was, 'How is the Church failing in our cities?'

3
We Never Did It That Way Before

The churches' failure to respond

Failure in evangelism

The apparent irrelevance of Christianity to so many in our cities suggests a failure on the part of the Church. However, it quickly became clear to me that in many cases the Church is not even trying to evangelise in these areas.

Cities are important

Mission can be divided into two categories. First, there is the traditional mission to people who are geographically distant from us. The second category of mission is to people culturally distant from the church, but living under the shadow of its spire. However large the numbers of those unreached by the Gospel in the traditional mission fields, it seems likely that there are many more millions on the churches' doorstep, in the cities.

The existing churches will not reach these huge and rapidly growing populations without cross-cultural mission at home. The unreached groups include indigenous people who are unused to, and alienated by, traditional church culture, language and worship forms. Then there are the new ethnic and linguistic groups who are changing most of the cities of the world. Finally there are the diverse sub-cultures of commerce, industry, the night, the deviant, the derelict, the alcoholic, the five-star international set, and many more.

These groups do not live by an eight-hour working and sleeping cycle, and can be reached only by shifts of pastors working around the clock. Too often this kind of outreach is not available: churches have exported their cultural patterns around the world. A Baptist Church in New Delhi fronts a busy street, but it is shut all the time the crowds are there. The mosques and temples are open but the Baptist Church remains shut until eleven on Sunday morning.

We have seen how cities force cultural and political change on their countries. They are also increasingly multicultural and multi-ethnic, and the various groups keep in touch with their countries of origin. For instance, 28 refugees from the Marcos regime become Christian believers in Chicago. A big wedding is arranged at which their entire clan will assemble, so they charter plane seats and fly home to share the Good News with their families. Christians reach aliens in Chicago, and people in the Philippines hear the Gospel!

Youth With a Mission recruit Yugoslav Christians from Zagreb, Yugoslavia, to work in Stockholm, Sweden. Their most effective ministry in the whole of Europe – including their own country – is with the 50,000 Yugoslavs there. Yugoslavs are becoming Christians in Stockholm and returning to their own country to share the Good News with their families and friends. Because of this kind of activity, the multiracial cities have a strategic importance in world-wide mission.

McDonald's Coptics and Burger King Baptists

However, when the Church does move into a city, too often it shirks the real challenges. A good analogy is the fast food outlets which are franchised worldwide from their parent company, and trade standardised products under a standard logo. When McDonald's moves into a new market and gives the local community a taste for hamburgers, it is followed by Burger King, which hopes not to create a new market, but to attract a proportion of McDonald's customers to itself. The new product is much the same but the company must persuade the public that it is different from, and superior to its rival.

The major denominations behave much like this. For instance, Egypt is a Muslim country where mission is difficult. 'We are forbidden by law to preach to Muslims, so we work with Greek Orthodox members,' a Baptist mission secretary once told me. It is much safer and easier to reach Coptics and turn them into Baptists than to attempt to reach non-Christians.

The denominations have gone into the Middle East with

their outside funding and marketing strategies only to compete with the denominations already there. They will do a little evangelising, but mostly proselytising – getting as close to McDonald's as possible. These strategies cause a great deal of unrest in the communities where they are practised, but are not reaching the unreached.

When the missionaries first went to the Philippines, they found 7,000 islands, so they did the sensible thing. They divided the islands among the denominations. Some were Methodists, some Baptists, some Anglican, and so on. But when they reached metropolitan Manila, all this changed. There you may find several churches in a row, all competing with each other, and the pastors feel that they are franchising. They treat people like clients and expend most of their pastoral care in trying to hang on to people who might be stolen by some other group.

In my own community there are 37 churches, and I have estimated that only one-fifth of the population has been reached. The other four-fifths are completely 'unchurched', secular and uninvolved. There is little point in Christians trying to reach other churches' share of that fifth. We can always find alienated members to pull from their own churches to add to ours, but this is not evangelism.

Typically, denominations are responding to the decentralised, multicultural churches of the United States and Europe by franchising standard, competitive outlets. Colleges are hamburger universities in this analogy, and the ministry product, like the hamburger, tastes the same in Miami as it does in Manchester. The training of pastors too often consists of running them through the hamburger university and giving them a quick placement by way of preparation for taking over their own franchises.

Two-thirds World pastors who serve in communities which are mainly Islamic, Buddhist or Hindu may recognise that Christians are in the minority; therefore they ought never to build up their own churches at the expense of, or in competition with other Christians. Tragically, in so many of these situations the pastors stop evangelising non-believers and find it much easier to proselytise others who name the name of Christ. A better strategy would be to pray and work together for the renewal of all the churches and do the genuine work of an evangelist. God still works miracles!

It is understandable that pastors and missionaries become defensive when faced with the realities of the city, but it is especially tragic when they are so unaware of the cultural bias of their own church model that they assume that it must be spiritually superior to any different denomination.

Financial dependence

A further problem may be financial: the urban church is kept dependent on a specific denomination by its funding. My pastorate of a poor urban church showed me the benefits of outside resources, but I also know that poor churches need to be freed from the bondage and imperialism of the churches who fund them. The pastor who serves his community, but is paid for by (and therefore accountable to) the denomination which sponsors his mission, resembles all the other professional workers in the community.

Churches or mission agencies perpetuate dependent ministries through the way they finance them. Paternalism, by outsiders of whatever nature, usually ends up using the community rather than ministering to it. Pastors empower the urban poor only by being accountable to them, including being paid by them. Pastors, with their backs towards their congregations and their hands outstretched to receive outside funds for their work among the very poor, are perpetuating the link between poverty and powerlessness.

Aristotle argued that some people are naturally 'born slaves'; the Spanish missionaries to the Americas in the years after Columbus adopted this thinking, and claimed that the natives of Spain's new colonies were inferior and incapable of self-rule and leadership of the church. When urban clergy or denominational officials speak of their mission to or work among given groups of people (the poor, the elderly, the immigrants, etc.) as though they were targets of mission and forever the objects of care, they are perpetuating this thinking.

Failure in training

Missionaries or pastors

When we turn to consider the training, attitudes and position of professional Christian leaders, we may learn from the missionary situation. There is no longer any valid distinction between missionaries going abroad, financed and organised by the foreign mission boards of the denominations, or by missionary societies, and pastors working in their home countries. It sounds harsh and radical to suggest that separate boards for home and foreign mission are now obsolete, but this is the new global reality.

Churches who have been sending missionaries to India and Pakistan for centuries now need help in working with Indians and Pakistanis when they come to London. Yet in my own denomination the home mission boards scarcely talk to the foreign mission boards. Latin America has come to the southern states and we do not even know how to talk about it. The United States is now the fourth largest Spanish-speaking country in the world, having more Hispanics than 23 countries of Central and Latin America, but the denominations still separate work in Houston as 'home' mission, and work in Mexico City as 'foreign' mission.

The rural missionary

Having established that our urban pastor will nowadays need the skills in linguistic and cultural adjustment once entirely the province of the foreign missionary, we may learn from the problems inherent in the missionary situation.

Missionaries are still mainly recruited from small towns and villages, and work in rural areas when their training is completed. A study of Western missionaries going to Two-thirds World countries found that nine-tenths of them came from small towns and villages. The Southern Baptists have 3,400 missionaries in 105 countries, mostly from rural backgrounds in the southern United States. It is not surprising that most of these missionaries end up in rural situations abroad.

There are several reasons for this. Firstly, it is generally cheaper to live there. Secondly, it is assumed that this is where the unreached people are, since churches are already established in the cities. The third reason is perhaps the most important. Missionaries have been trained in the language and culture of the specific people to whom they are going. When they approach tribal communities overseas, they have spent years studying the anthropology, languages and cultural patterns of their hosts so that their communication of Jesus Christ will not be offensive or unintelligible. Because of this, the villages represent the easiest way to penetrate the culture. By contrast, cities are complex communities containing a variety of faiths and cultures, which the missionary is simply not equipped to tackle. So missionaries often stay in rural areas where they feel 'at home' and confident, avoiding the complicated pluralism of the cities.

Foreign mission boards do not prepare their staffs adequately for work in the cities of their host countries, and home mission boards give little special training at all. It is no wonder that Christian professional leaders, whether they be styled 'missionaries' or 'pastors', are least trained and effective in urban societies whether at home or abroad.

Even where missionary societies are present in foreign cities, they tend to adopt a 'headquarters' mentality. They base their national or local headquarters in a city for the comfort of their staffs and to make use of the banks, the airport and the telex, but they do not minister to that city.

There is no integrity in this. Bangalore has one of the milder climates of India – and 200 church organisations. Miami houses the Latin American World Team, the Bible Society and many others ministering in Central America. They have Spanish-speaking staffs and use Miami to reach Latin America – but when I visited, I could not find one family who lived among the Spanish communities in the city itself.

You can see why societies pick Quito, Ecuador, for their headquarters. It is on the equator with a wonderful climate and view, and it is possible to live like a king there on a low salary. The city itself is a mission wasteland with the missionaries isolated in compounds. The refusal of missionary boards to understand the cities where they base their headquarters is a major barrier to evangelism in those cities.

The equivalent at home is the pastor who does not live in the same urban neighbourhood as the church he serves. He cannot be intimately involved with the life of his people unless he lives as one of them.

The question is – who loves these cities? Empire-building and flying the denominational flag is implicit in a theology which sees the city only as a mission field and not as a place to love others. Jesus wept twice in the Gospels, once at the death of his friend, and the other at the foreseen death of Jerusalem. If I do not love my city, I cannot work effectively there.

Training the urban pastor

I have painted a sorry picture of the missionary societies' behaviour in the great cities of the world. That of the theological colleges and denominations in the traditional 'home' countries of North America and Western Europe looks little better.

Professional church leadership comes overwhelmingly from the existing professional classes which are located in suburbia and small towns. Ministers are given the tools to interpret scripture, spending hours studying Hebrew, Greek and Old Testament history. What tools are urban pastors given to interpret the city – courses in social psychology, urban politics, cultural anthropology or urban history?

Two features of standard theological education should be delineated. The first is that it generally offers standard prescriptions for the situations a trainee pastor is expected to encounter. This is how you preach; this is how to do a pastoral visit; here is how you run programmes; here is how you do this and that. Pastors are not given methods of diagnosis – the capacity to survey, observe, analyse and interpret either their complex multicultural communities or their churches. Prescriptive training follows from the concept of the pastor as manager of a franchised hamburger outlet referred to above.

Diagnostic training equips the pastor to 'custom build' his ministry around the realities of the community he is serving. Instead of offering a standardised food product, he will study the local food needs of the community; identify the deficiencies in the local diet; and design a new food product for those people either not being served at all, or served badly.

The second feature of theological training links with this prescriptive training for managing standard outlets. All environments are seen as culturally neutral. All that the colleges need to do is to pre-package formulae of ministry which will do anywhere. So much theological education is middle-class culture with a smattering of the Gospel. What students are given works only in cultures similar to those in which their professors live and work. The lecturers teach theology from their middle-class contexts and values without even realising it. Theirs is a local theology all right – small-town and suburban. I learned this when I was living in inner Chicago and commuting to Trinity – a very conservative theological college set in a suburban Garden of Eden. I was daily struck by this disjuncture of environment, and knew that environments were not neutral.

The so-called practical courses of the colleges are taught without regard to the varied contexts within which the new skills may have to be practised. Biblical and church history studies are equally detached from their contexts, and from comparisons with the present which would enable students to identify with their backgrounds and processes as real people and communities.

Pastors have been sent out without effective answers to these questions:

What is the Church – people or structures?
How do I develop local leadership?
How can I bring in my expertise without intimidating the local people?
How do I identify and overcome barriers to communication?
How can the old core of faithful folk be renewed for new mission?

How do I handle the diversity of languages and social groups?
Which comes first – evangelism or community-building?
How do we care for special groups – the elderly, bereaved, broken families?
How do we initiate dialogue with suburban churches?
How do I cope with community problems?
How do I cope without support systems?

The effects of failure

This fundamental lack of training sends out pastors ill equipped to cope with the demands of urban problems. Many feel alienated and frustrated. Communication in the city, with its hundreds of casual relationships, is like pastoring on an escalator, where you need a great deal of energy just to stay still. This is painful for pastors who feel they have given up their own culture and civilisation to live somewhere alien; they have sacrificed yet they do not feel respected, for they are not 'successful'.

In London the word I kept meeting was 'fear'. Ministers' problems had overwhelmed them. Some churches in London's dockland – where they are faced by the decline of the traditional communities and massive redevelopment – had absorbed so much pain and so many problems that they seemed to have lost sight of the Lord.

Many urban pastors are lonely. Some hold multiple jobs to keep their families together financially. Others feel that their own denominational leaders have not understood the demands being made upon them. Some experience family trauma or walk close to the edge of 'burn-out'. Others clearly are not well themselves, incapable of real ministry.

One of the enticing routes out of these frustrations is the adoption of an authoritarian style of leadership. Some of the blame for this lies with the colleges which encourage competition for good results – and good churches. Young pastors celebrating their higher education may adopt authoritarian impatience, and walk all over the feelings of people who have kept the church going for years.

Sadly, some aspects of church growth theory – informed as much or more by management theory as by the scriptures – argue that churches grow best or fastest if their leadership is authoritarian. We should not be surprised how often new ministers come into churches to undo what is there, and plan new things, without consultation, consensus, or any democratic values.

The slide into authoritarian styles can be seen among the Christian leaders in any major city. The styles have little to do with the Gospel, but reveal a lot about the way urbanisation affects our personalities. Authoritarianism ministers to the needs of the pastor to be important and decisively in charge. Pastors may no longer gain personal satisfaction, growth and meaning in small communities of primary relationships, so they steadily alter their styles and goals in authoritarian directions, as ways of coping with the erosion of their power and status in their communities.

Frustrated feelings of marginality and inferiority may be accompanied by the false lure of authoritarianism, and then follows 'burn-out'. The pastor may move to a simpler, more familiar environment which he understands; or have a nervous breakdown; or decline into depression and the loss of all effectiveness.

A British pastor described how he was 'dumped' on a dreary estate characterised by apathy, unemployment and petty vandalism. Trying to manage all these problems caused him to 'burn-out' – an all too common experience. He began to turn inward and blame himself, and suffered guilt feelings. Until then, he had not realised how much 'cultural baggage' and paternalism he was carrying. Sometimes it is good to be stripped of these, but at that time the pastor was left feeling naked and helpless.

A London pastor said,

> I do not feel personally and temperamentally suited to the inner city but I have made a deliberate decision to return there. I spent three and a half years in an inner-

city area, and this nearly broke up both me and my wife. I have now spent nine years in a small college town and I feel that I am ready to return and have another crack at the city. There is the constant hazard of burn-out, more so than any likelihood that people are invigorated by urban work.

Very few British pastors spend their entire working lives in inner cities. A large church organisation found only four out of 142 candidates for church livings who described the inner city as their priority. Inner-city pastorates are difficult to fill. Those who take them may expect to be 'rewarded' by comfortable suburban livings when their duty is done.

Cairo – an example

Visits to seminaries or colleges of theology in the Two-thirds World show the pattern repeated, for the same fundamental reasons, sometimes complicated by the particular location. Those seminaries tend to be bastions of Western teaching and influence. For example, a few years ago I visited the Coptic Evangelical Seminary in Cairo, where 38 students were enrolled, none of whom originated in Cairo. The pedagogy and perspective was clearly Western and Reformed.

Later at a Cairo pastors' consultation with 58 pastors, including many from this seminary, several realities emerged through the discussion. Firstly, most Cairo pastors came from rural or suburban areas and did not understand the city. Secondly, in Muslim cities Christians are second-class citizens, minorities in a powerful Muslim culture. To gain status Christians encourage their children to enter business, medicine or the arts. Only the children who fail in these professions enter theological training, and so church ministry has no status.

Thus many Cairo lay Christians are professionals (physicians, business leaders, professors and pharmacists), and the clergy feel that they do not have the respect of the congregation. They compensate for their feeling of alienation, as minorities in the Muslim context, by becoming increasingly authoritarian in their pastoral styles and strategies. They tend not to trust their lay people. Most admitted that their seminaries and their synod or denominational leaders did not understand these dynamics and failed to help them cope.

The fear of change

White fright, white flight

I returned as a pastor to Chicago in 1965, and just as I came the Church passed me by. It was leaving. The evangelical establishment fled. They all claimed to have the Holy Spirit, the Word of God, and the Gospel, and at the same time condemned those who had any sort of social involvement. They concluded that the Church should not seek to save or renew social structures. The people who make these statements usually live in safe, reasonably healthy communities which benefit their families, precisely because they have good schools, stable economies and decent housing. These are the only people who can afford to say, 'Just stick to the simple, clear presentation of the Gospel to individuals,' because the traditional social systems are working for them.

Theological talk about the salvation of structures may be nonsense (I must admit that you cannot evangelise what you cannot baptise), but if Christians think that social and economic structures matter enough for them to move to where they function, they cannot criticise other Christians for working to develop or improve those systems in their communities where they do not function well.

Middle-class Christians in their comfortable suburbs are feeling increasingly fearful as they experience the consequences of internationalism on every hand. There is evidence that the urbanisation of the suburbs and rural communities continues rapidly. Twenty years ago, talk about drugs, crime, bad schools and unemployment branded you as an urbanite. Even five years ago, a talk to residents about urban poverty brought knowing glances and responses such as, 'Aren't they really just lazy?' or 'Isn't it true that they would rather be on welfare?' Public opinion has changed quickly as more and more suburban areas encounter what the cities experienced years before.

I began to wonder at the cultural captivity of the churches I knew. When the white middle classes left the cities, the churches went with them. So many evangelicals are unreconstructed social Darwinists who believe that only the powerful and the strong should survive. We have seen the large-scale commitment of evangelical churches to a conservative ideology masquerading as theology. We are seeing increased polarity of Christians on political and social issues. White churches and politicians abandoned the cities together.

The Holy Spirit did not leave. The fastest-growing churches in the northern American cities are black, and the Roman Catholics and the churches of many ethnic minorities are still strongly located in the cities. But too many Christians, fearful of the changing urban environment, moved away – too far away to be of any use in showing Christ's love to the city.

Museum churches

Luther advised each great Church council to study the issues of faith and culture in its generation, and so must we. Some groups have complete sets of concrete, cultural practices which they regard as almost synonymous with the Gospel. Their witness to Christ is frozen into cultural forms which are irrelevant or unintelligible to most people. They become museum churches with period lifestyles, music, dress and vocabulary. Evangelism for these believers carries all this cultural baggage. The way to the Cross is through the door of their tradition.

Churches create 'climates' and establish cultural boundaries around their churches. The congregation all wear suits, and the pastor in the pulpit asks people to come to Christ. What is the boundary? 'You can come to Christ but you must all dress like us.' I saw churches in India with full car parks and walls around them. The pastor is preaching 'Come to Jesus,' but the behaviour system of the church is saying, 'We are not of this community, you can come to Christ if you are of our social class.'

The ushers may also provide indications of the boundaries. If they are all white, middle class and smartly dressed, they may seem to welcome only those who are successful in those terms. Dress, cars, the architecture and location of the buildings, the time and language of the services, all show that while in theory everyone can come to Christ and worship him together, they really will not want to unless they look and behave like them.

Christians in these churches fear change; they interpret all change as loss, and they cannot bear to forfeit one particle of their tradition for the sake of outreach. The true Christian retains the purposes of ministry but alters or discards the forms when they no longer serve these purposes. He does this without trampling other people's sensitivities in the name of the Gospel.

Impersonal programmes

Another kind of fear is the fear that the church is dying. A pastor with this fear often panics, and reacts by setting up a lot of programmes in an effort to save it. He becomes a future-only pastor, and this is a dead end. He also ties all his church people into these programmes so that they have neither time nor energy for personal ministries. They draw their friends from church networks. We must liberate people from these programmes and encourage them instead to build their bridges of friendship so that their own networks begin to flourish.

I began my Chicago ministry with programmes. If they could bring in the millennium, it would be brought in! I had that church hopping with programmes. The problems were that they wore me out, were not very effective for evangelism, and cost a lot of money. A large number of busy people enjoyed being together, but there was no real mission.

I began to apply the lessons of the Vietnam War to the churches' methods for evangelising the cities. The United States adopted an impersonal strategy for the Vietnam War. The Vietnamese had been fighting the Chinese for a thousand years; the French for a hundred; and they defeated the United States in ten. I began to study how America was fighting the war.

They intended to humble the Vietnamese with aerial bombing. Americans parked their planes on Guam and flew at 37,000 feet in cosy, American-built cockpits; they bombed people without ever having to look at them or hear their screams. They gassed them or threw napalm at their villages and then flew back for a good night's sleep. It cost billions of dollars. It substituted technology for people on the ground, and it lost the war.

At the same time the churches were employing a similar strategy in the cities – and losing as well. All the congregations had moved out, and so in we came with a Billy Graham crusade to gather 50,000 people in a stadium to hear the Gospel of the one who became flesh and dwelt among us. We used media, radio and print, and blitzes of all kinds on television – anything except getting to know our neighbours.

We ran door-knocking crusades. I became convinced in the 1960s that this too was a dead end, and that as we had lost the war, so we were losing the cities. We must flesh out the Gospel by having Christians deliberately and strategically moving into the run-down neighbourhoods. There they can make relationships and share the Gospel. The bigger the city, the more personal we must become.

I am stressing the opposite of high-technology, expensive solutions. The fear of living in a changing church should not deter Christians from making primary relationships with neighbours who may change the church even more!

Barriers to urban mission

During my meetings with pastors all over the world I ask them to define the 10 basic barriers to the effective evangelism of their city. Until I had done this exercise several times I had thought that the barriers were in the environment, for instance, the persecution of Christians by Muslims in Cairo or by Marxists in Belgrade. I expected pastors in Mexico City to describe the difficulties of evangelism with the vast growth of population, and those in India to complain of the poor image of Christians as portrayed in films.

However, this was not so. I found from my consultations that most of the barriers are internal and may be summarised as, 'We never did it that way before!' – the Seven Last Words of the Church.

In Cairo, for example, the barriers they identified included the synod, church politics, egos which had to be massaged, and budgets and other bureaucratic checks which stopped them doing what they felt they should be doing.

Belgrade is on the drug route from Turkey, and has a large drug problem. When the Marxist government offered the churches a building and funds to run a drug rehabilitation centre, they refused the offer. They did not know how to cope with it and did not want to. They regarded it as a diversion from 'preaching the Gospel'. Another door had been opened and closed again; another opportunity missed.

The lists of barriers produced in cities as diverse as Copenhagen in the First World, and Cairo and Mexico City in the Two-thirds World, have all been similar to the following list which emerged in Belgrade, Yugoslavia, (Second World) in August 1983.

1. There is not enough organised prayer in a city of 1.4 million people.
2. We have too few properly trained leaders, both pastors and lay.
3. Most evangelicals lack vision, motivation and a burden for the lost.
4. Churches and pastors have a rural mentality.
5. We fail to use the opportunities for witness that we are given.
6. The Christian community lives as though it is in a ghetto, and Christians lose their non-Christian friends.
7. The churches do not co-operate.
8. Christians live busy lives and have many church meetings.
9. There is a generation gap between the existing leaders who are mostly over 55, and the emerging leaders who are under 30. There are few leaders in the churches between 30 and 45.
10. We lack suitable buildings and facilities.

The church leaders I meet want help to address and overcome these real barriers to the evangelisation of their cities, which are usually not perceived by denominations or outside missions. Nearly all barriers are created by church politics, policies, priorities or personalities, and not by the big, bad city itself. We will reach out to the urban masses far beyond the existing churches only when we understand what our barriers are.

It is not now technical resources and money from outside which will overcome these difficulties, but personal involvement and a willingness to change established patterns. We need to alert the church leadership to the needs of the cities and the problems, and then we need to train them appropriately. And to train the clergy, we must have a suitable theology. This, then, is the next step: towards an urban theology.

4
A Theology as Big as the City
An outline for urban theology

I had studied the nature of the modern city, and I had seen that the Church seemed unready for the challenge. I was being driven to find out whether there was a biblical theology for the cities. Here I was, a rural boy having a tough time in a tough neighbourhood, without any theology adequate to inform me why I was there, whether I should be there, and to guide me in what I should be doing.

Like many Christians, I had memorised Bible verses which confirmed my own views and experience. My colleges had taught me that theology was environmentally neutral, and emphasised what the Early Church believed rather than how it behaved. What I could not do was practise an avant-garde urban ministry and then invent an urban theology to permit it. I wanted to think theologically about everything the Church is and does, and to separate the externally valid work of ministry from its passing temporal forms.

My experience paralleled that of Luther when he was confessing his faith difficulties to Staupitz. Staupitz recommended Luther to study the Bible, and he began to develop a theology that was to transform the world. I am not pretending to be the theologian that Luther was, but I followed his example. The way to reach the city is not through programmes but by being biblical people. The urban minister must first be able to interpret scripture, and then must have the tools to interpret his city, so that he can let the Word of God speak to his situation. Theology is God in dialogue with his people in all their thousands of different environments.

Developing a theology of the city is one of the ways of surviving in urban ministry. I am arguing in this book that of all the pastoral survival strategies for ministers, the most important is the development of a world view; an understanding big enough to see what God is doing in the urbanisation of his world and the internationalising of his cities. I believe that this theological vision is little understood or experienced.

I began to read the Bible and church history in a new way, putting the events and people into their contexts. I first took the basic Hebrew and Greek words for 'city' in the Bible. They are mentioned some 1,200 times, and refer to 119 different cities. I then studied all these references in their contexts to see whether the scriptures could be taken to be 'anti-urban'.

Places are sacred

We live in the age of the throw-away environment – 'This is a bad neighbourhood and I don't like it. Let's move to another.' I found the typical Christian view, 'I don't like the place but I love the people,' not to be adequate or biblical.

One of the themes of John's Gospel is the Hebrew concept of sacred place, which begins with John 1:51: Jesus said, 'I tell you the truth: you shall see heaven open and the angels of God ascending and descending on the Son of Man.' Jesus is deliberately echoing Genesis 28:12 where Jacob 'had a dream in which he saw a stairway resting on the earth, with its top reaching to heaven, and the angels of God were ascending and descending on it.' Jacob regarded the place of his dream as sacred and called it Bethel – Hebrew for 'house of God'. Jesus is here regarding himself as the sacred place. Then in John 2 Jesus goes to the sacred Temple and cleanses it; to the Well of Jacob in chapter four and to the sacred Pool of Siloam in chapter five. This motif of the sacred place runs right though John's Gospel, with a further principle that every environment where Jesus worked was sacred.

We can look at any place in London or Chicago as sacred because God is present and at work there. We can also look at any place as sacred to which we are called as Christians and where we minister. We cannot work in our city unless we love it – its architecture, sewerage system, politics, history, traditions and neighbourhoods. This theology of place helped me to love Chicago. One free Sunday I visited 22 churches in different neighbourhoods to celebrate what God was doing and how he was worshipped in the city. Until 1966 I felt overpowered by the city, and I asked God to enable me to love it. That revolutionised me.

God sees that cities have personalities and assets. For the urban Christian and pastor there can be no throw-away real estate because 'The earth is the Lord's, and everything in it' (Ps. 24:1), and that includes every neighbourhood. Cities are a proper focus for redeeming ministry because they are treated in the Bible as persons and families and as extensions of the people who live in them.

Ezekiel 16, which is a judgement on Jerusalem for doing 'disgusting things', bears some study in this regard. The chapter opens by saying of Jerusalem, 'Your ancestry and birth were in the land of the Canaanites; your father was an Amorite and your mother was a Hittite.' It goes on in verses 45 and 46 to say, 'You are a true daughter of your mother, who despised her husband and her children, and you are a true sister of your sisters, who despised their husbands and their children . . . Your older sister was Samaria, who lived to the north of you with her daughters; and your younger sister, who lived to the south of you with her daughters, was Sodom.' The whole chapter is written in the language of family just as elsewhere in the Bible people are connected to place or family: Paul of Tarsus, Simon of Cyrene, and Simon Bar (son of) Jonah.

It is only in our Western, Greek-style thinking that we separate cities from people. I want us as the Body of Christ – as Kingdom people – to think globally about God's urban Kingdom, to feel kinship with the pain, the suffering and the celebration of other places and the Church of Christ in them. I have asked some good Christians, 'Have you prayed for five minutes of your entire adult life for Mexico City, the world's largest city?' and the answer has been, 'No, I have never thought of it.' You can pray for your city in the terms of Ezekiel 16: 'London, your sister in the south is Beirut and its suburbs. Your sisters in the north are Manchester and Liverpool.'

Abraham prays for Sodom

Sodom is mentioned 34 times in the Old Testament and 17 times in the New. The story in Genesis (18:16-19:38) begins with Abraham's prayer for the city – a prayer of negotiation that if as few as 10 righteous people could be found, God would spare it. Some people wonder if it is right to pray for cities. They regard them as evil and are prepared to condemn them and preach at them, but not pray for them. So the first deduction is that prayer for cities is biblically authorised by this and other scriptures.

The second deduction is that there is a relationship between the presence of believers and the preservation of places. The Lord is willing to spare Sodom if 10 innocent people can be found. This is echoed in Jeremiah 5:1: 'Go up and down the streets of Jerusalem . . . find but one person who deals honestly and seeks the truth.' Jesus continues this principle when he calls Christians the salt of the earth – penetrating its garbage and corruption with conscience and compassion; and the light of the world – demonstrating social and evangelistic witness and influence.

Thirdly, the Lord distinguishes between Lot and the rest of the city. The Lord can also find you and your people among the millions of the city. You cannot get lost and isolated from God.

The episode in Genesis 19:30-38 shows – lastly – that original sin is in us, not in the environment. Lot leaves Sodom for Zoar, and then hides with his daughters in a cave. His daughters get their father drunk and he makes them pregnant. (Their children are the ancestors of the Ammonites and the Moabites. The latter are incorporated into the genealogy of Jesus through Ruth.) Jesus also stressed this in Mark 7:15. 'It is what comes out of a man that makes him "unclean".' I know that many people regard the city as a corrupting influence and move out to save their children. The Bible puts that in perspective.

Jonah and Nineveh

Nineveh was one of three capitals of the Assyrian Empire, and a theology emerges around it in the books of Jonah and

Nahum. The Assyrians were the most violent people of the ancient world – the Nazis of the Middle East. They repeatedly invaded other countries, brutally slaughtering their inhabitants. Four Assyrian kings are mentioned in the Bible, and the invasion of Israel by Shalmaneser in the early eighth century BC is recorded in II Kings 17. He besieged Samaria and captured the northern tribes, taking 27,290 Israelites into captivity. Samaria was resettled with people from the various cities of the Assyrian Empire, and they developed a mixture of Jewish and pagan religious practices. Their descendants were the Samaritans who feature in the New Testament and to whom the Jews were so hostile. The next Assyrian king, Sennacherib, attacked what was left of Israel at Jerusalem.

Jonah's ministry was during the reign of Jeroboam II (793-753 BC), and so it was perhaps 50 years after the fall of Samaria that God called him to go to Nineveh and tell the city to repent. It would be like asking a modern rabbi to go to Berlin and preach. 'Rabbi, I want you to go and preach to the Germans in Berlin and I am going to bless your ministry. I am going to make the German nation and Berlin greater than they were under Hitler.'

Thus God called to Jonah to preach repentance to Nineveh, and Jonah responded by setting out in the opposite direction. Jonah equated his patriotism with the will of God, just as some modern Western Christians hate communism and therefore assume that God does not love Russia, China or East Germany. They are motivated by hatred and wrap the Gospel in the flags of the West.

Whatever your views on the historical basis of the book, it is absurd to suppose that the Jews would include in their scriptures a story which nobody believed, to teach something nobody wanted to learn. The book's hero is a loving God struggling to get a message to a pagan foreign city. A major lesson from Jonah is that God's love extended beyond national boundaries, and that God wanted Nineveh to repent and receive his love and forgiveness.

God's first act was to cause a great storm to rage about the ship on which Jonah was escaping. The multiracial crew prayed to their various gods, but even when Jonah confessed that it was his fault and told them to throw him overboard, they were reluctant to do so. They were not believers but had compassion on Jonah – just as many social workers, teachers or policemen with no beliefs in God whatever have more love than Christians for the city and its people.

When the sailors had thrown Jonah into the sea and it had calmed down, they 'greatly feared the Lord, and they offered a sacrifice to the Lord, and made vows to serve him.' God reached those people despite Jonah, and a whole boatload of sailors believed in the true God.

Jonah got up out of the vomit of the fish and preached to Nineveh like this: 'Forty more days and Nineveh will be overturned (I can hardly wait!)' He omitted any reference to God's forgiveness, reconciliation or justice – but scared people into repentance. What Jonah preached was basically true, but there was no feeling there. When the people repented, he did not know what to do. He had no love for them so he left Nineveh and sat down outside it 'and waited to see what would happen to the city' – hoping to see its destruction.

Sitting in the shade of his little plant Jonah asked God to let him die, as Elijah had done in I Kings 19:4. He was angry with God for killing the plant, and God used this as a parable. 'But Nineveh has more than 120,000 people who cannot tell their right hand from their left, and many cattle as well. Should I not be concerned about that great city?'

This question still hangs over those modern Christians who minister in cities which they do not love, and who are unwilling to accept people and forgive them. The book pricks the conscience because it is about the superiority the Israelites felt to every other race – a feeling which led them to turn God's love, which was intended for other people, upon themselves in self-congratulation. Much of the church is in this condition today. We need to reread the Jonah story and see the theology behind it, of a God who is struggling to make us go beyond our boundaries, values, and natural affiliations to love the people he loves.

Exiles in Babylon

Babylonia overwhelmed Assyria and became the great power in the Middle East, continuing its assault on Israel and Jerusalem where the Assyrians left off. Between 606 and 597 BC Nebuchadnezzar attacked Jerusalem three times, destroying the city, killing many people, and carrying Jews into captivity in Babylon. The exiles were force-marched for 900 miles.

In Jeremiah 29:4 the exiles were told to interpret these experiences as God's missionary call to them and not as a personal tragedy. 'All the exiles whom I have sent into exile' (RSV) – God allowed Nebuchadnezzar to take them to Babylon as prisoners. They were both refugees and victims, and also people who had been sent.

Then they were told to invest in their new environment and put down roots there. 'Don't live as aliens in the city with your suitcases packed ready to leave as soon as you can.' Most Christians do not live like this, but endure cities in frustration, and dream about leaving.

The Jews were then to seek the *shalom* of the cities 'to which I carried you into exile.' *Shalom* is almost untranslatable, and the nearest we can express it in English is 'a just peace' or 'wholeness'. In the welfare of Babylon, God was saying, the Jewish exiles would find their own welfare. This is a startling command of God. The Jews hated Babylon. They were victims and their city was in ruins, and they were told to seek Babylon's welfare. Our natural impulse is to pray for our friends, families, ministers, churches. If we have any energy left over we may pray for our city. This reverses the order of Jeremiah's letter, in which the welfare of the Jews depended upon prayer for the 'just peace' of their enemies. We are not entitled to read into Jeremiah's use of *shalom* only a reference to narrow Jewish interests.

The New Jerusalem

We end our tale of four cities with a brief mention of Jerusalem. If we want an urban theology showing God's love for cities we can look at the Bible's 1,100 years of its history. It is the city Jesus weeps over (Luke 19:41) and prays for (Matt. 23:37), and the New Testament ends with a vision of the New Jerusalem in Revelation 21.

The first vision of the New Jerusalem is in Isaiah 65. It is a text for pastors who are angry and have lost their joy. The redeemed city will have no infant mortality, and no exploitation in housing or marketing. People will live a long time and fully enjoy the things they have worked for. The work they do will be successful. Isaiah 65:17ff is God's blueprint for a redeemed city. If God's Spirit is motivating us truly, we will seek to implement God's agenda in our city.

> Behold, I will create new heavens and a new earth.
> The former things will not be remembered,
>   nor will they come to mind.
> But be glad and rejoice forever in what I will create,
>   for I will create Jerusalem to be a delight
>   and its people a joy.
> I will rejoice over Jerusalem
>   and take delight in my people;
>   the sound of weeping and of crying
>   will be heard in it no more.
> Never again will there be in it
>   an infant who lives but a few days,
>   or an old man who does not live out his years;
>   he who dies at a hundred
>   will be thought a mere youth;
>   he who fails to reach a hundred
>   will be considered accursed.
> They will build houses and dwell in them;
>   they will plant vineyards and eat their fruit.
> No longer will they build houses and
>   others live in them,
>   or plant and others eat.
> For as the days of a tree,
>   so will be the days of my people . . .
>
> (Isaiah 65:17-22).

Ministries for cities

Priests in the Old Testament were ministers in cities, where they were required to live. Priesthood was an urban institution and 25 types of urban ministry can be identified in the historical books. Priests ran cities of refuge and had responsibilities for public health and the eradication of plague. Their office was as much to do with pastoral care as with sacramental duties. Priests cared for families which had broken down, and were educators of the young.

A young man going away on military service was instructed to move his family into the city. The city would take care of the family and act as a substitute parent during his absence. The priesthood would have the pastoral care of these families.

Prophets, meanwhile, were extra-territorial. They might live in cities but could go to mountain-tops, deserts or rivers.

We need both kinds of ministry in our cities: a sacramental, pastoral ministry in the heart of the city – living with the people, sharing their lives, and building relationships – and also a prophetic ministry with a bigger perspective, to see beyond the city to the world.

Old Testament lessons for today

Moses – a pastoral giant

Stephen referred to Moses in Acts 7:22. 'Moses was educated in all the wisdom of the Egyptians and was powerful in speech and action.' He was bicultural, having been brought up in the Egyptian royal court with a superb education, probably including economics, law, architecture and mathematics.

The second phase of Moses' education is described in Exodus 2. He had a post-graduate course in the desert – God's university – with field studies in desert life, sheep-farming and public health in primitive conditions.

In the third phase of Moses' life the two aspects of his preparation came together. He took a group of rough brickmakers into the worst environment in the Middle East. During their 40 years in the wilderness he created a people with a history, a theology and a sense of identity, ready to enter the Promised Land and occupy it.

The range of challenges he faced resembled those confronting the urban pastor. The oppressed and uneducated people he led were often turbulent and angry. 'Why did you bring us up out of Egypt to make us and our children and livestock die of thirst?' (Exod. 17:3) 'Moses took his seat to serve as judge for the people, and they stood round him from morning till evening (Exod. 18:13).

It was only because Moses was teachable that he could survive burn-out. He accepted advice from his father-in-law, Jethro: 'What you are doing is not good. You and these people who come to you will only wear yourselves out. The work is too heavy for you; you cannot handle it alone. Listen now to me and I will give you some advice, and may God be with you.' (Exod. 18:17-19) 'Moses listened to his father-in-law and did everything he said.' (Exod. 18:24)

The advice was to train and appoint leaders. 'He chose capable men from all Israel . . . They served as judges for the people at all times. The difficult cases they brought to Moses, but the simple ones they decided themselves.' (Exod. 18:25, 26)

Numbers 11:10-16 describes Moses near the end of his endurance with the grumbling, whining people. He complains to God, 'What have I done to displease you that you put the burden of all these people on me? Did I conceive all these people? Did I give them birth?' The answer was for the Lord to reveal himself to 70 respected leaders chosen to help Moses. As his work neared its end, Moses enabled the old migrant group to pass on the torch to the new generation, and led the people to the edge of the Promised Land.

This is the greatest pastoral leader I know whose classical and field education occupied several decades; who took advice; trained leaders; delegated and built pastoral teams. He developed whole institutions for pastoral care in this appallingly hostile environment.

Joseph – economist and developer

There are 13 chapters about Joseph in the book of Genesis. He had an economist's career in Egypt and two seven-year plans, one for budget deficits, and one for budget surpluses. I was in Argentina once with a group including far-left and far-right 'flame-throwers' – those for, and those against liberation theology. I asked them to study the two passages telling this story (Gen. 41:46-57, 47:13-26), and answer the question 'Was Joseph a socialist or a capitalist?' They came back after a long discussion, still fighting. Half of them regarded him as a socialist, and half as a capitalist. Personally, I think that he was an eclectic, pragmatic economist using the structures of Pharaoh's Egypt to feed the entire Middle East. Why else are these 13 chapters about an economic developer included in the sacred text, in a hungry world like ours?

Daniel – sorting out faith from culture

Daniel was a Jewish exile in Babylon and was selected by Nebuchadnezzar's court to be trained as a court official. He was taught to read and write the Babylonian language (Dan. 1:4) and 'to these four young men God gave knowledge and understanding of all kinds of literature and learning. And Daniel could understand visions and dreams of all kinds' (Dan. 1:17).

When Daniel arrived in Babylon the temple in Jerusalem was in ruins, and the Ziggurat was the wonder of the world. By any norms of that culture, Daniel should have assumed that the gods of Babylon were more powerful than the God of Israel, whose temple had been destroyed.

Daniel moved into Babylon, learned its language and culture and became a leading political influence in the king's court. But he remained true to the God of Israel and 'resolved not to defile himself with the royal food and wine' (Dan. 1:8). This was an issue of faith.

How to distinguish between important issues of faith, and neutral issues of different cultures, remains an important question for modern urban Christians. We must also teach Christians how to learn the world's knowledge – science, humanities and ethics – without living the world's lifestyle, when that is detrimental to our calling.

Nehemiah – urban builder

After the Assyrians had captured Samaria and resettled it with their own people, they were overwhelmed in their turn by the Babylonians who destroyed Jerusalem and took many Jews into exile. The Babylonians were defeated by Cyrus of Persia in 539 BC, and 58 years after the exile the Medes and Persians became the great world power.

During this later time Nehemiah lived at Susa in Persia as a servant in the court of King Artaxerxes. He obtained leave from the king to go to Jerusalem to rebuild its walls, and he stayed there for 12 years. He was a great urban pastor. Chapters three to seven of the book of Nehemiah describe his organisation of the wall-building. Like all leaders of poor and oppressed people he had to motivate them against the ridicule and threats of their oppressors. He had to protect the weak from exploitation, and set a godly example to inspire those he led. 'The earlier governors – those preceding me – had placed a heavy burden on the people . . . . Their assistants also lorded it over the people. But out of reverence for God I did not act like that' (Neh. 5:15).

When Nehemiah had completed the rebuilding of the walls of Jerusalem he had another problem. Nobody wanted to live there! It would have looked like Berlin after the last war. Nehemiah rediscovered the tithe and applied it to people, urging families and villagers to set apart one family out of ten to move into Jerusalem. 'The people commended all the men who volunteered to live in Jerusalem' (Neh. 11:2). (The Hebrew word here is better translated 'blessed', which really means 'ordained'.)

I now include in my lectures on Nehemiah an appeal to people to move into one of Chicago's scarcely habitable districts, and some do respond. I challenge people to move into our worst neighbourhoods and to use their homes as centres of hospitality, especially near playgrounds where teenagers gather. This sounds like a radical strategy, but it is as old as Nehemiah. My college lecturers had stressed Nehemiah's personal integrity, prayer life and faith, but not his rôle as an urban builder and social planner. I studied his record for myself and found a striking, new and relevant urban theology.

Migrants and refugees

In a world where races are meeting and mingling as never before, it is important for Christians to seek God's teaching on multiracial societies.

Moses married a Midianite woman – Zipporah – during his exile in Midian, and in Numbers 12:1 he is described as marrying a Cushite (or Ethiopian) woman who would of course have been black. Miriam and Aaron criticised him for it, but the Lord was angry with them and said, 'How dare you speak against my servant Moses?'

The great movements of refugees and migrants are not just random occurrences in our modern world. We must interpret these massive, and often tragic human dramas from God's perspective in scripture. He is sending the refugees into the world so that they might advance his Kingdom in ways we would not previously have thought possible. Thus we must in no way disparage the unique experiences of migrants. Instead we must learn to see the Great Commission of Jesus to 'Go and make disciples of all nations' as something that God is doing, rather than something we are doing alone.

Seen from this perspective, Abraham and then Israel become models for modern refugees. Abraham is the 'father of many nations' (Gen. 17:4-6); Israel drives out other nations (Exod. 34:11) and is itself driven out and scattered. Paul demonstrated that God continues to relocate people throughout history: 'From one man he made every nation of men, that they should inhabit the whole earth; and he determined the times set for them and the exact places where they should live' (Acts 17:26).

The six centuries from the exile in Babylon through to the Persian and Greek empires saw the Jewish diaspora into every country and city in the known world. During this time the Jews had to struggle with issues of faith and culture. They developed new liturgies to express their faith. Synagogue worship was developed during this time and the scriptures were translated into Greek (the Septuagint). The decision to produce the Greek scriptures was a painful one. The Jews wanted their children to remember the old country and regard themselves as Jews, so they struggled to transfer their history and personal identity to the next generations growing up in very different circumstances. They had to decide how important language was to identity.

These changes were painfully experienced, but enriched Judaism and assisted the rapid spread of Christianity during the first century AD. Paul went everywhere with the Greek Bible.

It is difficult for the exiles to confront these issues of adaptation and change while retaining their faith; surely it is easier for the indigenous Christians to receive them with sympathy. There is much practical biblical instruction for Christians of host cultures, and for congregations ministering to migrants and refugees.

1. Strangers and aliens should be welcomed into our homes as Abraham welcomed the strangers in Genesis 18:1-8.
2. 'Do not ill-treat an alien or oppress him, for you were aliens in Egypt' (Exod. 22:21). This is addressed to individuals and to the state. It is not enough personally to treat strangers well, if our laws treat them unjustly. The Bible condemns us for tolerating injustice even if our personal conduct is just. 'The alien living with you must be treated as one of your native-born. Love him as yourself' (Lev. 19:34).
3. 'The earth is the Lord's, and everything in it' (Ps. 24:1). People may travel in it to escape famine or persecution. Abraham was a refugee in Midian, Ruth in Moab and Jesus in Egypt.

God's view of justice

I can refer only briefly to this vast topic, which has been the subject of endless controversy. In the Bible, at least 400 passages deal with social justice, of which Isaiah 58 is representative. Some 67 passages say in effect that the righteous state must ensure justice for the poor and needy. Josiah 'defended the cause of the poor and needy, and so all went well. Is that not what it means to know me?' (Jer. 22:16). We can also return to Ezekiel 16:48-50 for a comment on the destruction of Sodom. This is better known for its sexual immorality, but Ezekiel judged it because 'She and her daughters were arrogant, overfed and unconcerned; they did not help the poor and needy.'

Evangelism and mission have a companion: they must be accompanied by a struggle for justice and righteousness. God destroyed the Old Testament cities because they oppressed the poor and failed to protect widows and orphans. We must keep the urban poor high on our priorities. The poor are no less sinners than the rich, but they have also been sinned against. They are the victims of other people's sins and injustices.

It is only in our rich Western countries that we have the luxury of dividing two sides of a common coin – social action and evangelism. John Stott uses such images as the two belonging together like two blades of a pair of scissors, or two wings of a bird. Christians who are still debating these priorities often miss the point that social action is not done in order to communicate the Gospel, but as a sign or evidence that the Gospel has already been received and acted upon. Social ministry is the loving service of Christians set free from sins and bondage by the risen Lord.

The relevant Gospel

The mixed-race Saviour

The Good News according to Matthew begins with a cemetery tour in 1:1-16 – a genealogy in which five women are mentioned: Mary, and four of her ancestors. All four were foreigners and all had histories of varying degrees of scandal. Perhaps they were an 'historical support-group' to help Mary cope with the difficulties she was having explaining her pregnancy.

The first woman is *Tamar,* who was a Canaanite. Her story

in Genesis 38 concerns the elder brother of Joseph and fills a 20-year gap in the story of Joseph after he was sold to the Egyptians. Tamar married Judah's son Er, and after his death his brother Onan was supposed to marry her according to the Canaanites' complicated laws of succession. Since Onan refused to consummate the marriage sexually and subsequently died, Tamar was then entitled to marry Judah's third son Shelah, but Judah was afraid that Shelah would die, too, so he sent Tamar back to her own family. Tamar then dressed up as a prostitute and stood where she knew that Judah would pass to shear his sheep. They engaged in sexual activities and Tamar became pregnant and bore her father-in-law twins. One of these was Perez, an ancestor of David and Jesus. The text is so explicit that Puritans did not think it should be read from the pulpit!

Rahab's story is told in Joshua 2. She was also a Canaanite, a prostitute who ran a brothel in Jericho. Both James and the writer of the letter to Hebrews comment on her. James 2:25 says, 'Was not even Rahab the prostitute considered righteous for what she did when she gave lodging to the spies and sent them off in a different direction?' Hebrews 11:31 also says, 'By faith the prostitute Rahab, because she welcomed the spies, was not killed with those who were disobedient.' She was included in the family tree of Jesus as the mother of Boaz, Ruth's husband (Matt. 1:5).

Ruth herself was a Moabitess, and thus descended from Lot's incest with his daughters described in Genesis 19. This was the time of the Judges – Israel's Dark Ages. In this time Elimelech and his family fled to Moab to escape famine. Elimelech's two sons married Moabite girls, but the three men all died, leaving Naomi and her daughters-in-law. This story is the closest we have in the Bible to an episode in a soap opera, with women crying and saying goodbye. Ruth returned to Israel with her mother-in-law and married the most eligible bachelor in Bethlehem. He redeemed her and her land, and they had a baby. The key to the story of Ruth is in the list of names at the end. Ruth is the great-grandmother of David and an ancestor of Jesus. God moved through Israel's Dark Ages to produce a King and a Saviour.

In II Samuel 11 is the account of David's affair with *Bathsheba*. It is an all too common story – a man in his late forties with a mid-life crisis. He was left at home as Chief Executive while his officers fought the war. It was a long time since he had written any songs or slain any giants, and he was bored. So he had an affair with Bathsheba – who was a Hittite, a member of a warlike tribe – and made her pregnant. Now that he was in trouble and exposure and scandal loomed, he mounted a Watergate-style cover-up in three stages. The first was to recall Bathsheba's husband Uriah from the war and send him home to his wife, so that everyone would think the baby was his. Uriah did not go home to her. How could he go home to eat and drink and sleep with his wife while the other soldiers were at war?

In the second stage David got Uriah drunk and sent him home but again Uriah did not go. The third stage is a dastardly plot which we can hardly associate with the mind of God's chosen one. He ordered Joab: 'Put Uriah in the front line where the fighting is heaviest, then retreat and let him be killed.' David could then do what he wanted to do; marry Bathsheba and earn the good wishes of the nation at the same time for supporting the poor widow of a national hero.

The question for us is why these four women are listed in the opening of Matthew's Gospel. The infancy stories were the last part of the Gospels to be written, and it is notable that the Early Church was so committed to the resurrection, ascension and future coming of Jesus, that it had little to say about his earthly life. It was only when the Gnostics claimed that Jesus was a purely spiritual being that the Church reached back to remember and recover the infancy stories and identify Jesus with his roots and family connections – roots which include Canaanites, Moabites and Hittites.

Matthew equally relates the early years of Jesus to particular places, and recounts his political exile in Egypt; as President Anwar Sadat of Egypt put it in 1976 – 'The Christ Child fled to Egypt and lived in Cairo to escape the scourge of Zionism in Palestine!'

According to Early Church tradition, Matthew became a pastor in Syria, and his stress on these foreign women had a pastoral reason. He was trying to convince the Syrians that the Gospel was not just for the Jews or for people living in the Promised Land. Matthew's account includes the visitors from the East, and he ends his Gospel with Jesus' instruction to his followers to go into all the nations and make disciples.

These stories have a powerful appeal to poor city people whose own lives may be disordered or immoral. Here a Gospel for sinners is demonstrated, and I often include in my preaching these scandals in the ancestry of Jesus. Even Moses' mother is a great heroine with mothers who live on welfare. She floated her son down the river, got him rescued and then was paid to bring him up. Until I began to pastor fatherless families I never noticed these stories very much.

Matthew's text condemns racism in any form. On his human side Jesus got his blood from the world, as well as shedding it for the world. We are saved by the blood of the mixed-race Saviour of the world. I am helped to understand what John meant when he said 'He came unto his own', because now I know who his own are.

What Jesus did

We must preach the humanity of Jesus as well as his deity. He was a political refugee as a child, and as an adolescent and young man spent six years in the carpenter's shop for every one that he spent in ministry. He had a borrowed birthplace and a borrowed grave, and in between he had nowhere to lay his head. Your poor people will hear this gladly, just as his poor people heard him.

The story of salvation begins in a garden (Gen. 1) and ends in a city (Rev. 22). The purpose of God is not to return to the garden but to go on to the restored city. Jesus began on the periphery of Jewish power in Galilee where he had a large and successful ministry. There is no doubt that Peter and the disciples wanted Jesus to remain in Galilee, and would have preferred themselves to remain there after the Ascension.

Jesus however went resolutely to Jerusalem – the centre of religious, economic and political power. He entered the city in triumph, as a Roman general would have done, but instead of an army and vanquished leaders in chains he had his ordinary followers, and he was riding on a donkey. To symbolise his conquest he exercised his power in the Temple – the centre and symbol of God's rule in the city. It took only four days for the centre of power to crush Jesus, but it was there that the new community of Jews, gentiles, Parthians and Medes would begin the process of healing and restoring mankind.

Jesus' public style of ministry is summarised in Matthew 9:35: 'Jesus went through all the towns and villages, teaching in their synagogues, preaching the Good News of the Kingdom and healing every disease and sickness.' Sometimes Jesus preached repentance first, and at other times he healed blindness and leprosy or fed the crowds before any offer of forgiveness or preaching. He is seen in prayer for the city of Jerusalem as he foresees its destruction (Matt. 23:37-9).

Jesus was a trainer of disciples who were to build his Church and proclaim the kingdom of God after his execution and resurrection. He sent them out in pairs, and instead of writing a book 'chose them to be with him' (Mark 3:13). Sangster said, 'Christianity has something to be taught and something to be caught.' This catching of ministry comes when pastors share their ministry and give it away.

Notice how often the people who confronted Jesus resembled urban people of today, like Nicodemus, the rich, well-born, brilliantly educated orthodox Jewish public leader of John 3, with whom Jesus used the teasing metaphors of water and wind.

In contrast was the Samaritan woman to whom Jesus spoke, revealing that he knew all about her and accepted her (John 4:4-42). The woman was ready to believe and to follow him. Jesus then stayed with the Samaritans, entering into their world. They were regarded by Jews as socially unacceptable, and to seek the woman's society was socially deviant. What would such a style of pastoral evangelism look like today?

The woman became an evangelist in her village, telling everyone, 'Come, see a man who told me everything I ever did. Could this be the Christ?' (John 4:29). Many more Samaritans believed Jesus because he stayed with them and they heard his message for themselves. Jesus had a long perspective because he knew that he was going to send the disciples to Samaria later. At his ascension he instructed them to witness to him there (Acts 1:8).

We have already seen the ability of urban people to 'tune out' in order to cope with the psychological overload caused by the pressures of urban life. This is a God-given gift, but it must not stop us being sensitive to human need in the way Jesus demonstrated in Mark 5:21-42. This is a story of two fathers and two women – one a rich man's daughter who had lived for only 12 years, the other a poor woman who had been dying for 12 years. Jesus was pushing through the crowd at the request of the young girl's father, but he could distinguish the touch of someone who wished to approach him in faith, from the normal pressure of the crowd. He then healed the woman and said, 'Daughter, your faith has healed you.' By using that word he was telling her that she was somebody, and he identified himself with her as her father. He was able to respond sensitively to the need and faith of an individual, despite the pressure of the crowd which thronged about him.

Paul – urban missionary

Paul's work in the Early Church was entirely urban, centred on Antioch, Ephesus, Corinth, Jerusalem and Rome. As in the case of Moses, most theologians concentrate on what Paul said rather than on what he did. Paul always worked in teams which included Luke, Epaphras, Tychicus, Aristarchus and Demas. But Paul as an urban evangelist 'followed the contours of the urbanised Roman Empire', and the congregations to whom he wrote had many problems in common with our churches today. The urban conditions of Corinth and Chicago overlap to some degree, and I can find guidance in Paul for the parallel problems of my city. The Early Church was lucky to have Paul, an urban man from Tarsus, bicultural and bilingual.

Our review of his methods begins in Ephesus, the largest city in Asia, in Acts 19:8-10, probably about 51 AD. Paul's first three months are spent in the synagogue engaging the Jews in rabbinic dialogue. 'But some of them became obstinate; they refused to believe and publicly maligned the Way,' so every day he hired the lecture hall of Tyrannus and had *dialogoumenos* with the Greeks. He used what the Greeks called the 'socratic' method. Paul could switch from Jewish to Greek methods of reasoning, and from the synagogue to a lecture-hall.

Luke says, 'This went on for two years, so that all the Jews and Greeks who lived in the province of Asia heard the word of the Lord.' All Asia heard the Gospel because Ephesus was a great port city with a widespread sea traffic, and connected by the coast and river to Colossae and Laodicea.

The Gospel did spread to Laodicea, including to a wealthy landowner, Philemon, who we assume heard it from Paul during visits to Ephesus. He and Nympha are both recorded as running house churches (Phil. 2, and Col. 4:15).

In Corinth, Paul worked with Aquila and his wife Priscilla 'because he was a tentmaker as they were' (Acts 18:3). Paul ran his own business for 18 months. Tents were made by skilled artisans, from leather bought from the poorest people, and sold to the middle and upper classes. The tent maker had contacts with all the social classes. Paul also held discussions in the synagogue every Sabbath, trying to convince both Jews and Greeks.

Paul's story ends in Rome. 'For two whole years Paul stayed there in his own rented house and welcomed all who came to see him' (Acts 28:30). He was under house arrest in Rome but what he started there was essentially a community mission. Again we must admire Paul's creativity. He could not go out himself, so he created an urban mission team of five, who preached and brought people back to Paul. He is thought to have lived near the Via Appia in the Asian quarter.

Rome was the largest city in the known world and the only one with more than a million people. It was called *Caput Mundi* – the head of the world – and if all roads went there, so did all the sewers as well. All the refuse of humanity tends to flow downhill to the big cities. Among the human refugees who flowed into Rome, just as they do into countless cities today, was a runaway slave called Onesimus, and his story pulls together all the themes of urban mission.

Onesimus – from urban refugee to bishop: Paul preached in Ephesus in 51 AD; and the Gospel had spread to Laodicea by around 52-3 when the wealthy landowner Philemon was running the church in his house. Paul was in Rome in 63 AD, and one of his helpers there was Tychicus, who came from the Maeander Valley which flowed to Laodicea. The runaway slave Onesimus was discipled in Rome and became a Christian, and Paul sent him home to his owner, Philemon, with a 330-word letter which is included in the New Testament. He was probably discipled by Tychicus, who would have spoken the same language.

Paul relied on the good faith of Philemon. Under Roman law he could have branded Onesimus on the forehead with the letter 'f' for *fugitivus;* he could have executed him; or the third option was for Philemon to purchase the freedom for the slave and set him free. It was this last option which Paul wanted Philemon to take. Philemon's fellow-landowners would have wanted him to execute Onesimus as an example to other slaves, and you can imagine some evangelicals taking this line: 'Onesimus, would you just like to give your testimony to the other slaves? Isn't it wonderful – in just a moment you're going to be with the Lord.' In this way they could keep the law, evangelism would be done, and everyone would remain locked in the slave tradition.

Paul's letter is therefore a masterpiece of psychology. In verses 4-7 he 'puffs up' Philemon – he has heard of his love for all of God's people, and he has 'refreshed the hearts' of all God's people.

Paul then (v 7) reminds Philemon that they are brothers in Christ, and then describes Onesimus as 'my own son in Christ' (v 10). He is telling Philemon between the lines that he and Onesimus – his former slave – are now brothers in Christ. Then in verse 15, Paul says that Onesimus 'was separated from you for a little while so that you might have him back for good' – as a brother in Christ! Paul regards the running-away of Onesimus as having a divine purpose – as an action of God in the world. That verse is a window for me and gives me permission to speculate about why God is pouring people into the world's cities today. Are they only victims or is God accomplishing something? I do not want this to sound like insensitivity to the plight which these people are suffering, but as Christian leaders we must think about them theologically.

Paul is clearly asking Philemon in 17-20 to purchase the freedom of Onesimus and offers to pay anything owing – at the same time saying, 'not to mention that you owe me your very self.'

In this story evangelism has had drastic social consequences, creating the scandal of a socially integrated house church in which a slave – not a person but merely property according to the Romans – mixed equally with the highest social classes.

We move now beyond the New Testament to 110 AD, when Ignatius was pastor of the church in Antioch. He was taken prisoner by the Romans and marched to Rome to be martyred. Ignatius wrote many letters to Christians on his way to Rome, and the one to Ephesus was addressed to Bishop Onesimus! The conclusion of scholars is that this was indeed Philemon's runaway slave and that moreover he had replaced John, who was Bishop of Ephesus until he was banished to Patmos in 96 AD. If you were on the committee of that church, who would you think good enough to follow the beloved apostle and author of the fourth Gospel? It is all the more remarkable that an ex-slave should follow such a man in the chief church in the most important town in Asia.

In 59 years we have come full circle. We began in Ephesus with an evangelism strategy which led to Laodicea and Rome and ends back in Ephesus with a former slave established as the bishop. The Gospel bounced from city to city, and Paul was dead before the story ended. He did not see the big picture, as most of us do not, but this drama helps us to see the larger patterns behind our own urban ministry.

The Early Church – preaching out of misery

Many reasons are put forward for the growth of the Early Church, but one clear factor was its strong and attractive social ethic. It has been said that Christians did not preach out of success but out of images of misery, transforming them into love and fellowship. In Alexandria women rounded up destitute babies and orphans and cared for them. Christians in the Egyptian cities knocked on poor people's doors and offered to move in to nurse the sick, deliberately exposing themselves to illness.

The Letter to Diognetus said, 'As the soul is to the body, so are Christians to their city.' They shared their rooms and food, through not their marriage beds. They could not be distinguished by their speech or clothing but by their conduct and the quality of their characters.

Tertullian wrote in his *Anthology* in 200 AD, 'To no less a post than this has God called them, and they dare not try to evade it. We have filled up every place belonging to you – islands, castles, caves, prisons, palace, city forum. We leave you your temples only.' The Early Church related to its surrounding cultures at many different levels. We do not need new technologies to work in the city, but a rediscovery of this vision, energy and compassion.

The other theme of the Early Church may be stated thus: The entire history of early Christianity demonstrates the principle that the Christian is indeed a refugee on the face of the whole earth. The theme that his destiny is not of this world, that he seeks a 'Kingdom', that the end lies in the city of God beyond history, runs like a strong thread from Hebrews to Augustine.

By 250 AD the Roman Empire was losing its power and seeking scapegoats – as the Nazis did, and as some Western racists still do. Christians made great targets because they confessed that Christ, not Caesar, was Lord. During the persecution in African cities such as Carthage, many thousands of believers died as martyrs. Cyprian, the Bishop of Carthage, remembered that the Apostles had forsaken the Lord under pressure, and he forgave those who denied their faith when they sought forgiveness and entrance back to the

Church. However, for Novatian, a Roman Presbyter, Cyprian's reconciling action cheapened grace and trivialised martyrdom. The church split grievously over this and other issues. For Cyprian, Christianity meant love, forgiveness and reconciliation above all, while for Novatian, it meant maintaining truth and credibility under worldly pressure.

Both of these positions have their own truth, and yet urban churches are faced with similar divisions all the time, because pastors fail to see the issues clearly and to appreciate the long-term consequences of their actions. Rivalries over this and similar issues divide Christians in most of our urban neighbourhoods. Truth must be balanced with loving reconciliation in our pastoral ministry.

The Early Church was divided also about the physical and material aspects of creation. This debate continues to influence Christians, as in the emphasis that divides social action and evangelism. Hebrew thought made no distinction between spiritual and material. The first chapter in the Bible shows God creating the material universe and the last book shows him recreating and cleaning up the world. The Saviour was wholly material and wholly divine in his person.

All this was scandalous to Greek thought, which could not endure the idea of God getting his hands dirty. Archbishop William Temple described Christianity as the most materialistic faith in the world. It alone integrates matter and spirit, sewer-systems and salvation, politics and evangelism. We must not separate these things if we are to practise a truly biblical ministry that God can use.

After Constantine had legalised Christianity, many godly believers were troubled by the triumphalism and materialism in the Church and left the cities to live and pray on mountains, by rivers or in desert caves. This emphasis produced, then as now, an escape theology which severed these believers from urban mission. Some, indeed, are called to the contemplative life, but the idea that it is more virtuous to leave the city and be alone with God, than to try to serve him courageously among the urban masses, can sometimes be very attractive to the timid Christian.

We can all be timid Christians, when faced with modern

urban conditions: the flight to the desert cave may have been more appealing than Constantine's city Christianity, just as the lonely commuter trapped in his car may feel more secure than he would walking home through a slum to a city address. But it is only by living in a city, with a theological vision for the city, that we can attempt to reach the city's people. In the following chapters I offer an account of some of my experiences in an urban ministry, and the methods and techniques I found most useful.

5
Build Decision-making Like Muscle
Exercises with an urban congregation

Congregation in crisis

When I began my ministry at Fairfield Avenue Baptist Church I had a congregation of 11 faithful souls. They had kept the church going for a long while, and although they were devoted to the idea of evangelism, I knew that as soon as we began to welcome newcomers in any numbers, there were bound to be difficulties.

I started with work outside the church. I grew up in an athletic family and have always been interested in sports, so I teamed up with two professional football players to form the Inner City Athletic Mission. We recruited Christian football players to challenge the gangs drinking on the beach to play football. We drew up lines on the beach, beat the stuffing out of them and then invited them to a barbeque. We really roughed them up and were known as the 'butcher priests'! It was interesting evangelism and seemed congruent with the way the city functioned during the era of the Vietnam War.

We recruited kids and formed leagues, took them on retreats, rented theatres for Billy Graham films, and had rock concerts on playgrounds. Christian men and women who were interested in sports moved into the city. We had people living with us all the time in those days. Basketball evangelism began to reach people whom the church was not reaching, and one weekend 30 gang kids came to Christ on a retreat. The next weekend I invited them to church and they sat on the balcony. During the prelude a Mexican kid began a fist fight with a Polish kid. Now you don't stop a gang fight. You just steer it down the stairs and stop the traffic. While I directed the traffic the boys continued to fight. Here they were, having just come to Christ, attacking one another; city kids have limited vocabularies, and fighting is a way of talking.

The church people stood there pouring out their hatred for these kids like the Pharisees confronting Jesus, and this became a crisis point for me. I was employed to do youth ministry by a church which would not accept the kids. The kids were racially mixed and had very different cultural backgrounds from the church people. They fought with their fists, but the church people were fighting with words, and for me this was the same.

The congregation were like the disciples in the little boat in the storm described in Mark 4:35-41. Jesus had been teaching good theology all day but in the storm they forgot it all. All they could think about was survival. My congregation had been reduced to a survival mentality through which they filtered everything I preached and said. They gave most of the church's money and ran most of its activities, but they did not believe that anything could change.

Unlocking the core group

How does the pastor enter the congregation? Many older churches are maintained by small cores of older people, and most of their leadership comes from small groups aged over 60. Urban churches have often lost the middle-aged, middle-class people who have moved up socially, and away geographically. The survival mentality is common among the ageing members who remain, forming the urban church core group. Please do not berate these members or blame them for what you think is wrong with the church. After all, these are the ones who did not run away when the going got tough, and without whom the church would not have remained.

I took trouble to get to know the congregation and interviewed each member separately. I asked them, 'How did you come to know Jesus Christ?' Each person had come to know him in a different way, and none of them during a morning service in the church. Yet they still wanted me to give invitations every Sunday for people to come forward and be saved. They had been conditioned to want something to happen but not to believe that it ever would, and this was reinforced each week when the invitation was given and nobody went forward.

This first question can unlock and affirm the spiritual experiences and pilgrimages of the church members. Jesus is the one door (John 10:7) but there are many ways to get to him. It is good to share these stories. It broadens people's understanding of how evangelism might be done today, when they have forgotten how it was done yesterday.

I then asked, 'What were the circumstances of your life when you became a Christian?' This question helped them to unlock their memories – often back to the First World War. Some of them had lived through two wars and the Depression without losing their faith, but did not see how we could survive now. They began to see that their faith had sustained them through equally difficult times.

My third question was, 'What have you enjoyed in church life over the years?' People recalled things which had long been forgotten or suppressed. The men in my church had run a Sidewalk Construction Company during the Depression, building concrete pavements for people for a few cents. They had also run a sports club.

These were social ministries that brought men together: now they were nervous because I was doing too much social stuff. Had I suggested out of the blue that we started a construction company they would have described the idea as crazy. They had in fact been involved in social action themselves 50 years previously, but they had forgotten about it. They were saying to me, 'Pastor, stick to the Gospel!' but that is not what they were doing then. As I listened to their stories I realised there had been a lot more pluralism, openness and vibrancy than people remembered. When I recalled these stories from the pulpit, the congregation began to be proud of what they had done.

Thus these second and third questions may unlock and affirm many things necessary for outreach, but which now would be opposed as radical, costly, unnecessary or unspiritual, by the same people who had forgotten that they were doing all of them personally two generations ago. Today's most conservative or reactionary members may once have been pioneers. Nothing that the pastor suggests will sound as radical as some of the things that the old members did, or their parents before that.

I concluded these interviews with the question, 'If you could wave a wand and bring about a future for this church, what would it look like?' This not only tested the commitment to the future, but awoke people to a vision of future possibilities.

As I went home after each of these interviews, I reflected on the pastoral strategy I would adopt for that person, and how the interview had helped my own thinking. I listed the gifts and resources of the congregation to help guide the direction of future ministry. After my interviews, I taped my responses and wrote them up. I planned to telephone people on certain occasions with specific information; or to tell them that what they had recounted to me was happening again; or that I would like them to meet someone whose present experience was like theirs in the thirties. I was always trying to link their memory with contemporary reality. When appropriate, I mentioned anecdotes from the pulpit – 'I met Harold the other day and he told me . . .' Reticence should not prevent you from doing this if you can say a good word about someone. I preached people if their stories illustrated biblical truth, and they suddenly felt good about the church.

Creating vision

People cannot think about the future if they do not have memories. I call this 'having a functional memory'. We had monthly celebratory dinners, which helped people to remember for 30 days – a good start. We talked about what God had done during the previous month, and I reminded people about things which had happened. Eventually people learned to recall a year between annual meetings and began to think about the future and respond from their reserves of memory. Each church has a unique identity, and if people know this and feel secure in it, they can unlock commitment, direction, courage and compassion. Only when the congregation is able to set priorities will it offer the pastor guidance, and make him truly accountable to the church.

The urban poor live in the present and the pastor cannot develop leaders and point them to a happier, more hopeful future until he has helped them to create memory. The prophets constantly told Israel to remember the great acts of God in the past. Memory traditions are often built around symbols, and urban pastors may forget this. The pastor too becomes entirely pragmatic and overwhelmed by the tyranny of the immediate, and becomes a victim himself.

In a sense, time is a function of class. Blue-collar workers and the poor cannot invest in the future because they cannot control it, and they have lost their memory of the past. You do not unlock such minds with brilliant planning or stirring appeals to move ahead, but rather by reminding people of their achievements, and preaching like the prophets did about how God led us in the past – until it sinks in. The people will hear the call to future planning then and not before.

When you do call for commitment to new visions or tasks, it is wonderfully affirming for you, and the others, to report that the task is not so new or radical to all, but is similar to what the church did in the past. This provides a kind of parental permission for the old-timers, and becomes very reassuring when the pastor is asking the current generation to take risks. New pastors may discover that they are about the same age as the children of the church's older group. While you may assume that you are a mature professional by training and ordination, your core group may regard you as a youth who needs their parenting. You need to recognise these rôles and dynamics and try to articulate them.

When a church has reflected on its history and decided what it has done well over the years, and what have been its gifts to the community, new themes will emerge from the past. Only a congregation which understands its historical identity and mission can afford to risk changing its programmes. Pastors can change things by external force, without understanding, but then they may destroy traditional loyalties without putting anything in their place.

Vision is the critical issue. Kennedy told a story about a group of pessimistic kids locked in a room full of marvellous toys. They said, 'It's no good. As soon as we get to like these toys they will take them away.' The group of optimistic kids were locked in a room full of horse manure. Their reactions were quite different. They dug into it enthusiastically, saying 'With all this horse manure around, there's got to be a pony in here somewhere!'

Empowering the people

As the congregation grew I decided to live on a public aid salary like that of the church people, and refused assistance from my denomination. My Home Mission Board would have paid me, but our activities would then be a result of their funding. They could broadcast to the world everything that was going on as their achievement.

I could not pastor to people who were not paying me, because that would have been turning my back on them. Their powerlessness would have been reinforced if their pastor had been paid by, and accountable to outsiders. I scrounged and taught classes in college and seminary, and my wife gave piano lessons, so that we could stay with this group without receiving external funds.

Like every other helping profession, contemporary ministry teaching and practice increasingly draws its values from the culture of professionalism, rather than from biblical or historical sources. This can lead to the Christian life and ministry being seen as a performance by professional church staffs who do the ministry for the people. Pastors may have a psychological need to retain skills and information for themselves, or may lack the pastoral discipline of routinely investing in others. The results are similar – pastors do the work for the members and their congregations remain passively dependent.

I argue for an entirely different approach in which you give ministry away. The urban setting requires a wide range of human skills and spiritual responses available round the clock, and this is more than can be provided by heroic, pastoral 'Lone Rangers'. Pastoral teams are needed, and these must be created within the congregation as well as by assembling teams of professionals.

Involving other people in church administration and worship calls for planning and organisation, and the pastor must develop his personal discipline to cope with that. Jesus' pattern of training was to have people with him, and we must imitate it. He lived among the 12, the 70 and the multitude, and never manipulated, nor over-protected his colleagues. He did not, for example, exempt them from the physical risk of drowning (Mark 4:35), nor from the psychological fears which followed his execution. Picture the disciples hiding in an upper room behind locked doors eight days after the resurrection (John 20:26).

On the basis of this thinking, I decided that I was the pastor and the church members were the ministers. They would share the Gospel in their worlds of relationships and I would help them do it. They needed to learn confidence, vision, skills and decision-making. Empowering people does not always seem efficient to the trained professional, but it is effective.

New skills

I began by instructing the Church Secretary not to type the church bulletin. 'You are to teach other people how to type, so that they can get better jobs, and they can practise by doing the bulletin.' The bulletin sometimes went this way and sometimes that, and there were a few misspelled words, but it was the product of the members, and each issue bore the names of the women who had done the typing. Suddenly there was pride in the bulletin, and they were glad to give it out on Sundays. The most beautiful picture I saw in the bulletin was of an ugly fire hydrant. In America there are fire hydrants in the streets, and in the summer the kids open them and make fountains. So Ruth Robinson drew a hydrant with the words, 'The Kingdom of Heaven is like an open hydrant in the summer'!

The Church Secretary took a long time to understand my philosophy. She could have typed the bulletin in half an hour, but instead it took much of the week. She had to convene a group of women and let them practise on old manual typewriters we bought at jumble sales.

Because our building was nearly 100 years old, and decrepit, we started building and remodelling classes for our community. When the congregation grew big enough to support me with a salary, we called a second person. He was our building expert, and we used the building to teach job skills – roofing, plastering, plumbing, boiler work and rewiring. The fact that the building was falling down was the best thing we could offer. We ran classes in the various building trades in the community and people came for 10-week courses. This was another way of empowering people. Our builder did not do any of the work on the church himself, but always taught a class.

Using staff

I have said that as a high-energy person I began my ministry with programmes. These wore me and the church out! I am not totally opposed to programmes now, but I changed my style to that of training people and helping them to open up and minister. I made an early decision not to work alone but to pour my life into other people – a ministry of equipping, motivating and encouraging.

Too often a new pastor rushes in with his programmes, and recruits students from nearby Bible colleges, first to supplement, and then to replace local people who cannot measure up to the requirements and expectations of the programme.

Good comes of this, to be sure, and I am not wishing to dissuade churches from the right use of such programmes or such resource people. Some urban churches can very usefully become teaching sites, but the change needs to be negotiated carefully with the congregation. When it happens, let it be in the spirit of the 'mission in reverse' style of the Shalom Ministry in Chicago. There it is clearly understood that the indigenous local lay folk are the teachers, and the visiting students who assist temporarily are in fact the learners, being taught by the poor how to pastor the poor. There is great integrity in that kind of learning contract.

Generally, however, it is a stop-gap solution at best, and may retard the emergence of local leadership even further, by contrasting it with the high commitment and skills of the temporary workers. Local people may respond to temporary staff by concealing their inner feelings because they cannot face the possibility of being hurt again by more 'rip-off' relationships. Pastors are often too impatient to wait for gifts to emerge as God gives them, and rely instead on recruiting the particular gifts that they think God needs for their church. In fact, the congregation can almost always provide whatever is needed for ministry in their own particular situation – the real difficulty is convincing them of their own power to act and make decisions for themselves.

Public decision-making

One of the earliest committees in the Bible was an art committee to build a beautiful worship centre. Moses appointed Bezalel and Oholiab who had 'skill, ability and knowledge in all kinds of crafts' (Exod. 31:3). Why did God give the gift of art to people who were roaming, hungry and thirsty, through a terrible desert?

Luther's congregation had manure on their boots till the day of his death, yet he understood how deeply they thought. He said that during the wilderness period the Israelites needed to know the God of structure and beauty. Luther did not deprive the people of their art forms as the Anabaptists had done, and realised that the poor need art.

Oppressed people – like the Israelites in the desert – look into themselves, blame each other, and see themselves as victims. They regard themselves as without worth and without hope. Beauty and order are especially important if these attitudes are to be reformed. We can use symbols, art and structure to give people hope. A woman pastor in my community took on a church which no man would take. She had only one person in her Sunday School and together they laid out a flower garden, to show people that there was new life there.

In our poor, mixed-race neighbourhood one of the first

things to emerge was an art committee. Leadership developed through this, as much as through the more traditional bodies.

Our church was built by Swedes who painted the interior off-white. The Puerto Ricans and other groups like a lot of colour, so the Art Committee painted four of the windows in various colours and left the colour schemes for a month. We then voted during the morning service and the colour which was liked least was then painted out. We studied the remaining three for the next month.

We voted again, painted another colour out, and then looked at two for another month. After four months we agreed to paint a one-inch strip of rose around each window. It had taken four months to reach a simple decision, and some of my friends thought this was absurd.

There was a similar procedure to decide which colour to paint the back porch – and bright red won, much to the consternation of some of the old-timers. We had the only red porch in the community, but the Puerto Ricans going up and down the alley knew we were making a step towards them. Colour is so important.

During the morning service we marched around the building, looked at those colour samples and voted as part of the offering. People made their contribution by voting, and when they voted red, we went out the next week and painted it red. This kind of public decision-making is empowering.

You build decision-making as you build a muscle – by gentle exercise. You use concrete, small, non-threatening issues to start with. People cannot jump from paternalised, welfare-state dependency to democracy in one stride. You must have incremental steps going on for several years to change the climate and build leadership. Our congregation had been so put down by social workers that they could not make decisions. We therefore took a long time to make corporate decisions in our church, and we made them by a very open process.

We were creating a climate where people could take risks. People who had almost all decisions made for them in the urban world were learning to risk making decisions by talking and voting in the church. Establishing this new climate is a very important element of pastoral strategy. Buildings, budgets and physical entanglements are not always barriers to overcome, so that spiritual ministry can occur in the city. They can be very useful tools to unlock decision-making. No individual or small group should decide for everyone else what should be done about the building. That would be a middle-class efficiency model inappropriate for most urban churches.

You will not achieve this changed climate if you decide that your priority is to get things done, and act secretly and quickly like a business executive. You then reinforce the dependence of the poor upon decisions being made for them by outsiders. In too many congregations the decisions are made by the pastor, or by the tiny group of office-holders, and the rest may never be told about them, or consulted in any way. Tearing down the local icons, or kicking the cultural props from under people by forced changes in their worship services, music traditions or church programmes seldom accomplish anything worthwhile.

If people are feeling insecure (and generally speaking, who doesn't feel that way in the troubled climate of the urban neighbourhood?), they will cling even more tightly to established practices in the church in the hope that it will not change.

Caring in the congregation

The CIA

In my first year I asked God for one man – and this is all I got. During the second year a second man joined. It took five years to get a discipleship group going in the church, but then we formed one a year, called CIA – Christians in Action.

We allowed leadership in these groups to emerge by turning certain middle-class assumptions upside down. One was that if you want to teach someone something, you charge them fees for your tuition, with the expectation that if they pay for it they will get more out of it. We decided that the time of poor people was too valuable for them to give it away. So in Fairfield Church we paid 10 people $100 to undertake a 10-week course of 10 hours per week. The congregation was investing in them and wanted them to learn some leadership skills. We budgeted $1,000 annually to CIA – a large proportion of the total budget of $15,000 at that time – and this told the people that they were valuable. This income especially helped women whose men were not churchgoers, and who resented the church's influence on their women.

The deacons in our church were five women and five men, and they would look out for people with emerging leadership skills, such as a single mother who was managing her household very well. The people were picked also from different racial groups. The deacons would then tell the person that they had observed how the Lord was working in his or her life, and offer an invitation to join the CIA.

There was an application form and interviews, as this was valuable practise for people who had to apply for jobs. We were choosing them, but we then asked them to go through a process of selling themselves and saying why they would like to be part of the CIA group. We selected people during the autumn, and around Christmas the 10 people would stand in front of the congregation for a consecration.

CIA training began in January. The church then invited 10 prayer-partners to come forward, one to stand by each person, and they made prayer contracts. They were to contact their partner each day for the next 10 weeks and ask one question: 'How shall I pray for you today?' We were training 10, with 10 others partnering in prayer. Then we identified 10 other people from the congregation with skills to teach – such as a Sunday School teacher, a carpenter, and administrative staff. I taught hospital visiting, reading scripture and leading worship. During the 10 weeks we gave them a lot of information and made them a kind of support group, in which they also had social evenings together. They were paid $50 after five weeks, and the remaining $50 after a further five weeks.

Each year we were training 10 more people in leadership

skills. In May we held a retreat in which the officers reviewed the previous year, decided what went well and what didn't, and what they would like to see happening during the next year.

Growth by caring

During my decade of leadership our church grew to 200 families and helped start seven Spanish daughter-churches. Many things began to happen – but not until my sixth year. Later our denomination had a 'Growth by Caring' scheme, but our congregation decided that it was doing this already. We wanted to be known as people who cared – for the community, for schools, for senior citizens and so on. We cared about Jesus, and when we looked at the people who were being added to our number, they were all coming in because we cared for them in some way.

We fed the poor, had an arson committee, a police committee, and conducted funerals for murdered gang-members. There were ministries to a group of alcoholic men, and a Bible study for 40 gays and lesbians.

We did not abandon impersonal contact either, and distributed leaflets in May with our summer programmes, and in September with our autumn and winter programmes. These leaflets were distributed round the entire neighbourhood to let the people know we were there.

The church developed many training approaches to help people minister to their worlds. We ran courses in counselling people who were under great stress, being divorced, or on drugs or alcohol. Church members would encounter these situations and needed help to deal with them. Because they were not very good readers I read books about these topics and ran classes on them.

Preaching dignity

During our church year I preached from the Old Testament from September to December, prefiguring the coming of Jesus. During the winter months of January and February – when the Chicago weather is at its coldest – I suggested we move from the large church, which we could not heat, into a basement room. This reduced our fuel bills and also gave us an annual wilderness period of reflection and planning. From Christmas to Whitsun I preached from the Gospels, and for the rest of the year from the Epistles. These are some of the ways I kept my pulpit ministry alive and structured.

I needed to give my people a vision of their own dignity and that of their work – whether in the factory, home or community – in the sight of God. I told them that the first picture of God in the Bible is of him getting his hands dirty making the world. Just as God made water, dirt and mud, so he created my congregation in his own image. Jesus was a manual worker, and they are like their Lord when they get their hands greasy working on engines. Luther preached to the peasants in Germany that all work – even potato-peeling in the monastery – was the gift of God; I told my people this as well. Work can be worship; even – or perhaps especially – jobs we regard as bad, like sewer maintenance or garbage collection.

When Luther translated the Old Testament into German in about 1524, he stood in the market place in Wittenburg for two weeks listening to the peasants, so that he could use their grammatical constructions in his translation. I remembered this in my own preaching. For example, I preached on Amos dressed as a farmer, and paraphrased the book into the language of a typical American farmer. I illustrated Amos 7:7-9 by walking up and down with a tape measure to tell them that they were all crooked.

I remember preaching on the lost things from Luke 15, because a number of families had lost their sons to drugs and other things. I started my sermon by sweeping the sanctuary with a broom for seven minutes without saying a thing. Meanwhile Corean was playing Beethoven's 'Rage over a lost penny.' The music ends with a crash and a bang, and just as she finished it, I found a lost penny under the communion table. When I held it up the people broke into spontaneous applause. They finally figured out what I was doing.

I have already mentioned cultural boundaries, and I was concerned to see that the worship did not exclude any group in the community. I was careful not to have everybody dressed in the same way, or only men in the offices. There would be a large mother on the platform, a Puerto Rican usher and someone playing black music, so that people could say, 'This is the church for me.' We had young people reading the scriptures, playing music and acting as ushers. The ushers were aged from 12 upwards, and even younger children handed out the bulletins. I wanted little kids to communicate the idea that the church is for little kids. Sometimes we would have a tiny child and an old man together handing out the bulletins. We were communicating what Jesus said; 'You can all come to me – not just rich people, white people, smart and good-looking people, but ugly people, hurting people, people of all races and colours.'

Celebrations

In my area we need celebrations. We held monthly People's Feasts to celebrate the fact that we had got through the last month. This was the time when we invited friends or family or the police officers who guarded our beat. 'We would like to have you as our guests of honour at our monthly dinner, to thank you for your work in our community.' There may have been alienation, but these functions gradually changed relationships. The church invited groups of people like this to its dinners and applauded and thanked them for serving them. Guests included factory owners, bar managers and other business people, and pastors of other churches.

Several years ago our church celebrated its eighty-fifth anniversary in Chicago by inviting the mother-church to come to a thank-you dinner. This was an old Swedish church, once the most significant church in this denomination in the region. Meanwhile, Fairfield's Spanish daughter church is as large today as the mother church was in the halcyon days of the Swedes in Chicago. The celebration was of a century of church life and growth in Chicago – or, How a Swedish-speaking mother produced an English-speaking daughter who produced Spanish-speaking grandchildren.

Witnessing out of tragedy

Some of our finest evangelists came to a faith in Jesus through personal tragedies. Let us take the example of a mother living on welfare, whom we will call Beverley. She had six children of her own by three different men, and an extended family of 50 with whom she was in close touch. She became a believer after the tragic loss of her sister's six children in a fire. She got to work with her group and turned out to be a great evangelist. She was like the Samaritan woman in John 4 who loved to bring people to Jesus. She was ready and willing to minister to her world, and so I helped her to take a fresh look at it simply by drawing diagrams.

Beverley was asked to list her extended family and put down one basic human need for each person. She thought of one dying of cancer, another on drugs, one with a broken marriage, or lonely, or a family struggling with a delinquent child. I then told Beverley, 'You are the minister of this network of people. This is your world. Choose five of these people whom you feel do not know Jesus but have a basic human need. You can't minister to all 50. Jesus only handled 12, and he lost one. You can't expect to do better. So I want you to think about how you could minister to them.' She was encouraged to think of very practical ways, sending letters of encouragement, going to a home and cooking a meal, or inviting the daughter of a sick mother to stay.

Beverley's second chart showed places like her launderette across the road. Several women went there daily to smoke, talk and swear about their husbands. This was her second world of relationships and I encouraged her to share Jesus with five people there also. Her third network consisted of the people she worked with two days a week at the Social Centre. Once her world was reduced to manageable proportions, Beverley became a powerful force for the Gospel.

Mary-Ann also became one of the most dedicated Christians in our church. She had married and divorced an alcoholic. One of her sons tried to slice his wrist because he was gay, and the other was shot and killed in the street in an argument over a parked car. Mary-Ann came from Tennessee, and was what we call a hillbilly. If you have dinner in a hillbilly house and you ask for the bread, you'd better get your hands up to catch it because it will come like a frisby! When this first happened to me, a kid sailed the bread from the far end of the table, shouting, 'Catch it, pastor!'

I visited Mary-Ann where she worked in a factory making plastic cups and plates. The women sat wearing ear-plugs and put pieces of plastic into machines to be stamped out. They had to shout at each other all day. Mary-Ann had told her work-mates that her priest was coming – their word, since many of them were Catholics.

When I arrived she gave me a big hug and a kiss and said to the others, 'You all, this is my pastor.' I told them, 'She is right, I am her pastor – but she is the minister. Her task is to minister to all of you. If you have any problems, you tell her. My job as pastor is to help her to help you.'

After that, people would ask Mary-Ann to help them in all kinds of ways, or to ask me to conduct funerals or pray for sick relatives. The people at work were not churchgoers, but just because I visited her there and shouted ineloquently over the machines, it opened up the gate to an impressive witness.

Mobile city

Our church was in a 'port of entry' neighbourhood, with many immigrants moving into very poor housing. After a few months they would leave. In one year, two-thirds of all the children in the elementary school who started in the autumn had left by the following spring. Sometimes the urban poor moved to escape landlords and unpaid bills, so they did not tell anyone when they intended to move. I would see new people in church on Sunday and when I went to call on them on Tuesday they had vanished without trace.

The community where I pastored was characterised by female heads of households, and children came from families where many men have come and gone. The only wealth of the poor are their children, and our church directory noted all the children under their different surnames. Some families had six different names. In one of our services a woman might get up to share her personal pilgrimage, and introduce six children by four different men, only one of whom she had legally married. But she had become a believer in Christ with her children. She was proud of them and willing to introduce them, and we as a church family were willing to accept them. They became part of our body, our family, our community.

When I worked with children I had at once to work with their parents; often they came from broken homes. Two-thirds of my congregation were women. I was also looking forward to when the child would grow up and form a Christian household. I was seeing not only one person, but three generations.

Many women in these circumstances see the pastor as a surrogate sex object. A strong male becomes a target in a community of shifting and inadequate men, and isolated women. Where there was a non-churchgoing husband he might resent the pastor because his wife talked about him frequently. Most of these women were craving for husbands, or for husbands who would love them. If the pastor is loving and caring he is going to get 'vibes'. This is one of the dynamics of ministry in the inner city. I made a covenant with two very bright women in the congregation that they would monitor my relationships with the other women. I also had a woman associate with whom I worked as a pastoral team.

One terrible drunken husband phoned me regularly and threatened to kill me. 'I'm gonna kill you, you bastard!' I always replied, 'You wouldn't do that, George, you're too nice a guy!' George's sons were churchgoers and would go home and tell him that he was drinking too much. George blamed me for the conversion of his wife and children, and for the threat I presented to him when his boys wanted to be like me and not like him. Children crave loving fathers, and if their fathers are not at home they resent that.

I made myself accountable to fathers when their children went to the church. I called to see them and said, 'Your son is going to our church. What would you like to happen to him?' He might say that the child cheeks his mother or does not show enough respect to his parents. I then agreed to preach on those issues and return later to see whether the father could report any improvements.

All kinds of sexual experimentation went on early among the children, and I had a 12-year-old mother whose own child was adopted by her mother. These things revolted and saddened me, but I had to start where people were and move them on to where they needed to be.

The search for solutions

I could not care for my congregation without being aware of their surroundings; so often social conditions affect the physical, emotional and spiritual state of the community. As I became more involved with the individuals who made up my congregation, I became more personally involved with their struggle. I saw the city as a series of interlocking systems, and itself within national and international systems. So many of the things my poor congregation needed were in the hands of the city, state, or federal legislatures. It was not enough to stand under the cliff catching the people as they fell, without going to the top to see who or what was pushing them over.

Redlining and speculation

A group called TRUST (To Reshape Urban Systems Together) made a study charting the cash-flow in typical Chicago slums, and published its work as 'Managing the Urban Dollar'. A major issue is redlining, a system which began in insurance and spread to banks – which in America are the main mortgagees of property, not building societies as in Britain.

A community is identified with a red line on the map as being unsafe for a 30-year mortgage. The banks stop investing in the area as blacks, Spanish and others move in. House prices fall, and the politicians reduce the level of public services at the same time. As property values fall, speculators move in. They have good lines of credit available to them, and buy up houses cheaply, subdivide them, and fill them with tenants. They can buy off the building inspectors, and exploit their properties until they become dangerous or ruinous. Buildings can then be fired for any insurance available.

We have seen this cycle time and time again. The people who have continued to live in the community then say, 'Tut, tut, look what these black people are doing to our once beautiful neighbourhood.' They are either unaware of, or unwilling to accept, the systematic evil perpetrated by the banks, politicians, and others who have set this decline in motion.

Often the city council invests in new areas, and enters the old communities only in remedial ways through the funding of social workers and programmes directed towards clients. These communities become served by outsiders with whom they have client relationships. The wealth which used to build the community has been syphoned off, and a new kind of funding creates a dependent community, a client relationship and powerlessness. All the decisions which affect the community are made elsewhere. Professionals are aliens and keep the community locked into dependence.

The banks continue to take the savings of the poor people, but they invest them in new areas. The poor are actually investing in their own demise, as their savings are channelled by the banks into financing suburban growth.

The franchised fast-food chains also move into poor areas to suck out the dollars like leeches. Some people will get fed, and a few kids will get jobs at minimal wages, but that is not the mission of the franchise. It is there to make money for a headquarters far away, and will close its outlets as soon as any further decline comes. By contrast, the locally owned shops circulate money up to eight times before it leaves the community.

In Illinois more than half of all money directed to the poor comes through the medical services, and hospitals are growing all over Chicago. Our local hospital – St Mary's – has single, carpeted rooms with colour TV and telephones. No poor person around the hospital is housed in such comfort, and the only way they can get the money aimed at them is to be ill!

At present the hospital beds are occupied by local poor people, but most of the revenue pays the huge salary bills for staff who live in distant suburbs. There is an armed guard on the car park, where theft, rape and assault occur regularly.

The staff live in nice neighbourhoods and think that they are doing wonderful work for the poor: they cannot understand these attacks. They cannot see that to the poor, the hospital is a symbol. The car park stands where homes used to be. The staff are not seen as benevolent individuals, but as part of a system which has oppressed the people and taken away their homes.

The Chicago Board of Education budget is larger than that of several European nations, and two-thirds of it comes from non-local (state and federal) sources. This money, too, aimed at the poor, flows straight to the suburbs where the staff live. A few kids get educated (though the public schools in the slums are very bad), but the education system's main functions are to attract federal money to the city, and provide employment.

Most of the other services are also labour intensive, and their chief expenditure is on salaries, which mainly go to people who live in the suburbs. We discovered that there is enough money being spent in Garfield, one of Chicago's slums, to keep two suburban communities in their prosperous lifestyle. The poor are being used as funnels to give money back to the middle classes. This kind of cycle perpetuates the powerlessness of the poor.

Political action

As I have said, one of my main concerns was how to empower these communities. Too often pastors deny that seeking to empower and stabilise the neighbourhood is the business of the Church. The behaviour of most churches is not easily distinguished from other commercial establishments in the city, and is not neutral in the processes which affect poor neighbourhoods. I have noted above that most pastors are paid from, and accountable to their denominations, and many live well outside the communities to whom they minister. The powerlessness of the community is a pastoral issue.

I wanted to act in a decisive way to break these cycles of exploitation. Part of my training was in Saul Alinsky's methods of community action. A Jewish radical, Alinsky believed that sin was real, locked into community patterns of discrimination. He argued that you have to 'get the visceral up'. The group must be encouraged to hate something or someone – a freeway going through the neighbourhood, a company or a landlord. The organiser's job is to organise the hatred, and if there is not an issue for the group to hate, he must find one.

One of the Alinsky-style groups I joined took a slum landlord to the housing court for rats, garbage accumulations and code violations. He was a prosperous lawyer speculating in real estate and owned 37 slum buildings. The landlord slipped some money to the building inspector and the violations continued. The tenants were afraid to act because of their fear of eviction.

So we took a dump truck, filled it with garbage, took it to the nice suburb where the landlord lived, and distributed the garbage all over his neighbours' lawns. We took a TV crew with us, and as we were arrested we shouted out, 'This is what your neighbour has been doing to us for years!' This was worth 30 seconds of prime time on TV, to make the landlord a social pariah on his own neighbourhood and turn all the neighbours against him.

If you accepted the principles of the 'just war' theory, then this sort of community action strategy could indeed be justified in my turbulent community at that time. However, I now had to consider whether there was not a 'more excellent way'. Before this drastic action we had attempted to reconcile the landlord to his tenants, some of whom were members of my church. We achieved a result in this case, but what had we gained? The tenants were evicted and the buildings closed down. It would have been better to have found a way of encouraging him to repair the building; or to have enabled the tenants to form a co-operative and buy it from him.

After a great deal of reflection I decided the Alinsky method was not for me. It was too adversarial and tore neighbourhoods apart. I and other social workers became angry all the time. There must be a better way. It seemed to me that personal contact was the answer – not just with the poor, but with the rich, the exploiters (whether intentional or unintentional), the bankers, council officials, the influential people. Out of personal contact come love and trust, and out of loving and trusting relationships comes a different sort of power.

6
Into the Community
Being an effective urban pastor

Caring for our congregation led us out into the streets around our church; the lives of our congregation were inextricably tied up with the social conditions in their immediate environment. And, of course, all outreach by its very nature takes us out into the community. Because of this, I came to realise that the urban pastor must be aware of the wider picture.

Interpreting the neighbourhood

How do you interpret a neighbourhood? First let me ask a parallel question. How do you interpret scripture? Most of us have been taught to look at a text in context. The single verse or passage may communicate powerfully and immediately by itself, but it usually helps us to relate it to the chapter and the book; to know what kind of literature we are reading; to know something about who wrote it, when and why. We need to apply the same principle to our neighbourhood. We can regard it as a specific text, or we can work to find out what makes the city tick and how that affects our community.

Urban neighbourhoods are not unrelated bits of geography that happened by chance. Some neighbourhoods – like some biblical texts – seem to make sense at first glance, but there is usually much more to them than meets the untrained eye. The functions of cities affect neighbourhoods and confront congregations with opportunities and restraints. If the pastor does not understand the larger urban picture, his daily experiences and local situation can overwhelm him. Because urban neighbourhoods are turbulent, programmes which worked well before may no longer be effective. Your entry strategy needs to include two approaches – the formal academic one, and the informal one which I call networking.

You should become knowledgeable about the history, people, politics, institutions and neighbourhoods of your city. This knowledge should be added to and deepened throughout your entire ministry. In the nearest university, college or polytechnic you will find theses and other studies on all aspects of your city, and on most of its communities. The council department where urban planning is done will supply plans and statistics for your area. If pastors see the bigger picture, it will help them sort out priorities when competing calls for time and money come.

You can classify your community by the communication into, out of, and within it, and by whether you can put a boundary round it.

1. A classic slum has identity, but communication into it is only via the media, and there is little communication out.
2. In a stepping-stone community the people are trying to get out. The population is on the move all the time and ministry is especially difficult.
3. A transitional community is undergoing change, perhaps racially, or ageing, or changing its class structure.
4. In a diffuse community there are few clear boundaries, no community identity, and only individual communication. A typical middle-class commuter suburb is like this.
5. A parochial community has very strong internal communication, but very little goes in or comes out. A neighbourhood may have several of these – often ethnic or other sub-cultures. They are reached by 'gate keepers' like the Big Mama in a black community. She runs the community and knows everything about it, and you can get access to it only through her.
6. In a healthy community communication goes on in every direction.

Your neighbourhood is likely to contain elements of several of these different types of community. It has its own characteristics and needs a pastoral style to suit them. The church will usually need a variety of pastoral styles if it is to reach all the varied elements in its neighbourhood. A practical assumption is that people join churches where some of their needs are met. So it is helpful to reflect on the various groups of people in your neighbourhood and identify for each a basic human need and an appropriate church ministry response.

For instance, a transitional neighbourhood might have these identifiable groups:

- Single career adults
- Retired and aged
- Institutionalised
- Commuters
- Ethnic groups (identify each group)
- Broken families
- Deviants (gangs, prostitutes, etc)
- Handicapped
- Students
- Professionals
- Public employees
- People living in high-rise blocks
- Middle-class dropouts
- People living on social security/public aid

Some of these groups will overlap, but listing them clarifies your thinking about approaches.

Networking the neighbourhood

Once aware of the spiritual and social needs of an urban area, where do we start? The pastor alone may feel helpless when faced with this complex pattern, and this is where the importance of personal contacts comes in. I suggest that pastors should invest one day a week in 'networking' their communities – building personal relationships at all levels. This can eventually build up into a city-wide network of people with influence.

When pastors have been asked why they do not investigate their community resources in a systematic way as they begin their pastorates, most reply that they do not have the time. On the other hand, others find they are too busy not to do this. The investment of time at entry brings returns when the emergencies come (and they do), and you find yourself able to cut through the red tape and go directly to the people who can help, precisely because you have invested in a relationship.

Networking the pastors

My first move was to meet all the other pastors. I visited 83 churches regularly, and 53 of them had services in languages other than English. I did not trouble myself with whether they were 'sound' or not, and always used the opening speech, 'My brother, my name is Ray Bakke. I am the new pastor of Fairfield Baptist Church, and I want your help. I'm new to this community and I wonder if you could tell me the most important lesson you've learned about being a pastor here.' I went to affirm my colleagues and learn from them.

I had some painful experiences. A Presbyterian minister said, 'You're a Baptist? You want me to tell you what a Baptist is? He grabs people on street corners and asks them whether they're going to hell.' At this point the minister grabbed and shook me! 'Then the fellow says, "No," so the Baptist tells him, "Well then, go to hell!" ' That was his understanding of who Baptists are.

By contrast I met Paul Knutsen of the Bethel Lutheran Church; we became close friends. I also made friends with other clergy and we began a clergy association together, and began to work on some of the community's problems.

You need not necessarily agree with your fellow pastors' theology to honour your calling and theirs by such visits. God's Kingdom is far larger than your own congregation. A question such as the one I used communicates respect for your colleagues in other denominations. It says that you do not see yourself as a new neighbourhood messiah, and therefore a threat to everyone else. You approach as a learner.

Some clergy will not want anything to do with you, but others will make the effort to build bridges. There is a hunger for fellowship, and quiet friendships can emerge to benefit you, your congregation and the community. Most communities have enough violence and conflict without you adding to it. We need both new ministries and the renewal of old ones, but the pastor labouring in an old church, nearly spiritually dead and kept going only by outside funds, may never meet the pastor who moves into the next block to start a new ministry. The two do not share their work; nor teach, nor learn from each other; each is committed to the validity of only a single pastoral strategy. They remain permanent threats to each other in the same urban neighbourhood.

I tell my students that I want them to be chaplains to the other pastors in the area and accept some responsibility for making other churches healthy by being encouragers and reconcilers. Your pastoral colleagues are reaching some people you will not, and your goal is to build up God's Kingdom, not your personal empire. We live in pluralistic communities and one church cannot do all the work alone. Our style should affirm the existence of other churches. In times of community tragedy or trauma (as in the riot seasons), you will need to stand and work together. Your network development at the very least becomes a kind of significant insurance policy. You may do some co-operative programmes eventually, but even if you do not, networking pays dividends.

This recognition of collegiality among pastors is important to their personal health and growth in the city. I must make it clear that I am not talking here about formal committee structures linking pastors, like Inter-Church Fellowship and so on. I remind you of the definition of network given at the beginning of this book: 'a group of people who relate informally'.

Difficulties: It is worth considering why urban pastors are so often competitive rather than co-operative.

1. Our time is fully occupied by hyperactive church programmes.
2. Many pastors are part-time workers, and it is not easy to arrange meetings with them.
3. Some congregations have doctrines or behaviour we find offensive.
4. We are kept isolated by our own feelings of insecurity, lack of knowledge, or other inadequacies.
5. We have various forms of 'messianic complex' which puts us in competition with other pastors and makes us intimidating to them.
6. The historic separatist stances of our denominations promote divisions and mutual antipathy. Many

churches in my own denomination are very suspicious of any ecumenical relationships.
7. Ethnic and linguistic diversity separate pastors.

I am urging pastors not to allow any of these reasons to deter them from making these networking visits. The list may help you to analyse your ministry situation and begin your visits right away. These visits should be at least annual, and sustained through early discouragements.

Lay ministry: Compassionate, Spirit-led, modestly equipped pastors often do fantastic ministry for God in cities with the Bible and little else. Many are lay folk who experience God's call to preach; they take a course or two in an evening school and they become some of the most gifted urban leaders. Much of their power comes from their life and service among people they know better and love more than anyone else. Please seek out these non-college folk, affirm and build bridges of friendship and co-operation with them, so each can learn from the other.

A first-generation leader with natural gifts may become defensive with a college-educated pastor from elsewhere, and the pastoral outsiders need to build bridges.

Your larger perspective makes your contribution useful, but not superior. Cities are torn by race, class and constitutional structures, and so are urban churches. We desperately need pastors who commit a significant part of their energy to the networking and building up of other church leadership, especially with those who come from other countries.

Networking social agencies

My second round of visits was to the public and voluntary agencies working in my community. Western cities are a maze of service agencies, including the following short list.

Public	**Private/Voluntary**
Police	Service clubs, Rotary clubs, working men's clubs, etc
Schools	Legal Aid, Citizen's Advice Bureaux
Welfare	Social Service organisations
Prisons	Food pantries, clothing banks
Courts	Shelter programmes
Hospitals	Halfway houses, women's refuges
Political groups	Special need programmes
Offices of City Hall, council, etc.	

There are probably many more of importance in your local area. I visited everywhere from the milk delivery depot to the schools, identifying the key people.

Seeking justice: I went to court many times with members and families related to my church, and we listened to many cases where the poor were not given fair decisions by the judge. A neighbouring pastor who also did this got so frustrated at the obvious discrimination against the poor that he stood up to address the judge. He said, 'If it please the court, I have been listening to these decisions and must ask you, where is the justice?' The judge's reply was, 'This is not a court of justice, but a court of law. If you want to bring justice, change the law.' I have never heard a more eloquent statement supporting political involvement. Courts do not exist to provide justice, and law is not written by people who live in these districts. This is why the Church must lever for power politically, and why pastors need networks of peers like lawyers and politicians.

In Chicago we have 50 aldermen, and each has a section of the city. I went to see my particular one when he was newly elected, and invited him to dinner with the congregation. He was impressed by the love of the congregation and became a fast friend. He has a Catholic Polish background, and came to a Bible study and experienced a conversion like Luther's. He is now Deputy Mayor of the city, and one result is that I now have a pipeline to the city hall of which I would never have dreamed. Over the years he has given numerous lectures to my seminary students on politics, and how pastors and politicians can help each other.

Helping to serve: When you begin these networking visits, the approach is to introduce yourself and your job and say, 'I need your help. What have you discovered about this community? What are you doing here? How can I work with you?' I recommend that in the first year of your job as pastor you contact all the services and agencies you can. If the school is being vandalised, this is a matter of equal concern to the local residents and to the Education offices. Most of these agencies are divided, and officials may well be isolated. It is better to establish networks of peers than to hope that the various hierarchies will solve all the problems.

In most Western countries about half the social workers change over each year – talk about burn-out! They are the symbols of alienation and may be hated for the work that they do. They become do-gooders, caring for the poor but coming from middle-class college backgrounds, and often unaware of the racism and paternalism that they carry. Your rôle can have more influence than anyone else's in bringing social workers and other frustrated professionals – like the police – together to improve the services delivered to your community.

We all use the various services and should recognise them as 'God's common grace', when public transport runs on time, and the sewers safely carry away our effluent. Pastors need to know who to call on in emergencies. Because many urban people have no extended families and a huge percentage of the city may consist of single-parent families, God's good gifts include public and private agencies that care and serve. Churches can help create such remedial services where they do not exist, and support them where they do, and help a great many families thereby.

If pastors wait until one of their members gets into difficulties before visiting the agency concerned, they are taking from the community's institutions and leaders and not investing anything in return. There is no integrity in joining groups or building relationships just to take from them or to learn how to start up in competition.

Networking businesses

After the visits to clergy and social agencies comes a third round of visits – to businesses of all kinds, starting around the church building and working outwards. Visits to shops, newsagents, garages, factories or financial institutions may be viewed as courtesy calls on the people who serve the community and your congregation. Because your people work, shop, save or spend in these institutions, they will eventually involve pastors formally or informally.

You should meet shopkeepers, ask questions about the community and leave calling cards for subsequent contacts and emergencies. Some business managers who serve your people may in fact be dishonest or corrupt, and urban neighbourhoods seem to inherit more than their fair share of these. But do encourage the support of local businesses where possible, and invite factory owners or foremen to your church.

Be sure to tell the woman in the flower shop, the youth who sells newspapers or the man who hires a few local residents, that they are significant to the health of the neighbourhood. They are like the glue that holds things together. In this round of visits you may receive referrals eventually, especially for weddings and funerals. These can be very special opportunities for ministry.

If you encourage candour, you will learn all sorts of wonderful and terrible things about the church – perceptions very different from those of the congregation.

When I did this exercise, I visited 44 local businesses in my first year. These included groceries, one-man businesses, garages and mechanics. I went to bars because they are centres of fellowship for the community, where people gather to pour their hearts out over their drinks.

One pastor I know visited a bar and the manager complained about a drunken customer slobbering all over the bar and putting all the other customers off. The pastor reflected upon this, and offered the manager the presence of two people who would sit at the back of the bar in the evenings. When a troublesome customer came in the manager would say, 'Here is a caring team who are willing to listen to you.' The 'carers' wore distinctive jackets with logos on them. The pastor was a Southern Baptist, and the congregation found it hard to understand when he and other members came in smelling as though they had fallen into a barrel of bad wine. But they had more baptisms from the taverns in one year than from a decade of evangelistic missions.

Benefits of networking

I place a high priority on networking and suggest that pastors spend about a fifth of their time on it, regarding this as investment time. The same principle applies to specialised Christian ministries, like those with youth, though here the networking would be limited (a youth leader needs to know his colleagues and the agencies dealing with youth).

My summary of these three rounds of visits is that if you continue them steadily over the years you will come to know your community better than anyone else. The church must discover, and relate to, all the other churches, agencies and businesses in its community and know how they function, or it will always be marginal to urban life; the pastor will always be reduced to rushing in with ill-thought-out programmes which consume both his and his congregation's energy.

Before new strategies are designed, church leaders should explore what is there. It may be better to renew existing ministries, already rooted in given cultures or subcultures, than to bring in new ones. The average pastor or congregation can assist and strengthen the specialised services and ministries of others and refer cases to them. They are then left free to add those services which come from the special gifts and commitments of their members. Before spending your limited money it is wise to see the big picture. It is sad to see churches competing with each other, or with other agencies, to reach the same groups.

Surviving in the city

There is a further benefit to the networking concept: spiritual support for the pastor. While outlining the many avenues of activity, it is worth considering for a while the nature of the urban pastor's work and the hazards he encounters.

Ministry burn-out

Pastoral effectiveness, to say nothing of pastoral survival in the city, requires that we put some boundaries around our life and work. It is impossible to bleed for everyone for very long. Martyrdom where required is beautiful to behold, and not a few urban pastors have been faithful unto death, but martyrdom where not required shows foolish lack of wisdom and stewardship. There are several reasons for failure and burn-out.

Firstly, pastors are often equipped with prescriptive models which do not suit the community they serve. Because cities are diverse and dynamic the urban scene is not what it was a decade ago, nor is one urban area like another. Pastors superimpose old action models or traditional evangelistic missions and crusades on their people; often these are inappropriate to the realities of cities and the way people function within them.

The pastor needs tools to diagnose his unique situation, not a series of models which are unlikely to fit. Typically pastors measure their performance by the guidelines of efficiency and the numbers of programmes they are running. These are not appropriate ways of establishing boundaries and setting valid priorities.

Secondly, there is a variety of managerial hazards, such as:

treating church maintenance as mission;
using people for purposes which can be equated with the legitimate goals of the church;
adopting an authoritarian style;
being impatient with the culture and tradition of the congregation;
failure to delegate authority to staff and lay leaders;
insensitivity to the city's effect on people's lives.

There are also some peculiar pastoral hazards (noted by Sanford in his book *Ministry Burn-out*).[1] The minister may find:

his job is never finished;
he cannot always tell if his work is getting results;

[1] Arthur James Ltd, London, 1984

his work is repetitive;
he is always dealing with people's expectations;
he works with the same people year in and year out;
his energy is drained because the people he works with are always in need;
he mostly functions through his public image, while protecting his private person;
he may become exhausted by failure.

Fourthly, there are severe external forces in cities which lead to failure and burn-out. Nice people, compassionate folks and good pastors are ground up and spat out daily. As well as unjust structures and aged and decrepit institutions, there are the demonic powers, and Satan goes around like a roaring lion, seeking to devour and destroy.

Understanding conflict

Perhaps the most complex hazard for the urban pastor is that state which may be generalised as 'conflict'. The pastor is always in the midst of conflict and must be aware of this and be able to cope with it. Conflict can be regarded as normal in human society, and our task is to make it healthy for our organisation, just as in our bodies muscle and bone must be in tension if we are to be able to stand up. However, to make this tension healthy we must understand and use it, not merely become exhausted by it.

We may identify various types of conflict; firstly there is *environmental conflict:* this includes attitudes created by the environment, for example between generations in America over the Vietnam War, or between generations in Britain over the punk subculture.

There is *structural conflict:* an example of this is the conflict between the deacons (who want a ship-shape, orderly church) and those responsible for outreach (who may bring in others who threaten that order). Whenever these groups meet there is a war on, because they have opposite mandates. The pastor is caught in the cross-fire. Structural conflict can become personal if we do not diagnose its source, as indeed can all conflict.

Finally, there is *conflict of images* or ideology. One reason for pastoral conflict is that people have numerous different images of the church and the role of the pastor within it. There are nearly one hundred images of the church in the Bible, and I list 25 popular ones in Chapter 10. If the people identify the church as a sheep-fold, you become the rather paternal shepherd protecting the weak creatures going 'Baa! Baa!' A conflicting image is that of an army, with you as Colonel-in-Chief issuing orders to your disciplined and obedient troops.

Another problem arises between the understanding of churches as 'voluntary' organisations, and the pastor's need of, and training in, the 'culture of professionalism'.

If we do not identify accurately such sources of conflict, we will turn inwards and think that if only we prayed more, worked harder or studied more, we would be more effective. This leads to self-blame, defeatism and burn-out.

Conflicts can originate in the turbulent urban environment and push us into frantic activity, or authoritarian modes of control to compensate for the feelings of futility which result.

The pressure of the city is like the climate of a war, in which no one has time to stop and admire the flowers, or be considerate. Many urban pastors may be sociologically and theologically liberal in theory, and yet act with the crassest dogmatism and conservatism. Just as brutalised children often become brutal parents, so do pastors who fail to see how the city is affecting them, become brutish in their treatment of lay folk, and invite a conflict which they do not understand.

The pastor's priorities

Clearly with all these hazards and difficulties besetting the pastor, it is vital that he should have a clearly thought-out survival strategy. I suggest that your time should be divided roughly into five equal parts between the following tasks:

1. Preaching and teaching the scriptures so that people know who they are and what their mission is; this should be expressed in prayer and worship. This task includes your preparation and personal Bible study.

2. Pastoral care. This includes your congregational visiting, hospital calls, funerals, and working with committees to care for the elderly, the sick and the poor.
3. Administration. Planning, organising, budgeting, and the formal committees. This involves you in delegation, and in altering the climate of your decision-making so that more people participate.
4. Community-building. This includes networking and 'putting your arm around the community'.
5. Discretionary. This is the time that you can choose to allocate to different things. Perhaps you have a special interest in youth ministry, or are working on an academic degree, or doing a special study into counselling. Your personal educational needs are important. In some communities you may need to learn a second language.

The last fifth is a matter of negotation, and none of these categories is hard and fast, but for guidance only. However, if you spend, say, half of your time on personal pastoral caring, this is too much. The pastor must train pastoral teams to share this work. All too often the community networking and personal study and preparation are squeezed out by routine pressures. These are 'investment' times, and lead to an all-round increase in the pastoral effectiveness of the whole body, so you should not allow yourself to neglect them. The effective urban pastor is disciplined about time, but also disciplines himself to think clearly about strategy and priorities.

Only when pastors preach, teach and care for their congregation, and administer the church soundly, will they be free to involve themselves in their communities, denominations, or pressure-group campaigns. Whether or not we get approval and co-operation from our congregations to lead in untraditional ways depends upon how well we perform the traditional duties of the ministry.

The pastoral team

The 'Lone Ranger' is not a good model for the urban pastor. Moses had his 70 leaders and his Joshua; Jesus had his 12; Paul had Barnabas, Timothy and others; Luther had his Philip and Amsdorf. When Elijah burned out and was depressed enough to ask God for death, he was given Elisha so that he would never be alone in ministry again. Seek out your pastoral colleagues in the city; nourish the networks of relationships; and accept them as God's gifts to you for growth and renewal. To recognise and nourish these depends upon your having a Kingdom theology which can set your unique ministry and your distinctive church in a broader historical and social context.

Many churches have staff teams who may work full or part time. The urban staff team needs a balance of men and women to model the image of God: 'male and female he created them' (Gen. 1:27). It is very important in disrupted communities with many separated families and many mother-only households that the children see church leaders of both sexes working together. This wholeness gives them a vision of the family as God intended it.

Choice of staff: The purpose of the staff should not be to run the programmes but to be resources for multiplying the gifts of others. A strong professional staff, paid by and accountable to outside agencies will only increase the feelings of inadequacy and dependence among the congregation. I would like to see churches depend less upon outside aid for maintenance, including pastors' salaries, so that outside money could be channelled into mission projects negotiated on a partnership basis.

The choice of staff should depend upon the work which the congregation collectively wants done. If they have identified certain groups of unreached people, then they will appoint staff – whether voluntary or paid – who have the particular gifts and skills required. Staff in an urban church should always be accountable to the congregation. In traditional churches youth leaders, ministers or choir directors are usually the staff needed first, but urban churches might want senior citizens' workers, cell-group leaders, housing specialists, or a pastor with a second language.

The urban Roman Catholic churches have always maintained multiple staff ministries, with diocesan pastors and personnel from various church orders working together in a variety of ways. There is a great deal of wisdom in that approach. One wonders when other denominations will develop permanent mission orders so that gifted, called and trained persons can be placed alongside permanent pastors for urban ministry. Ironically, Protestant or evangelical groups do this in mission work abroad, but seldom at home.

Some college and university graduates, musicians, artists, sports and business people should be recruited and trained for urban living and ministry roles. Christian college students need to hear Nehemiah's invitation again. There are some large housing blocks almost inaccessible unless Christians move into them. There are playgrounds, parks and schools where Christians could build relationships and use recreation, arts or sustained friendships to put social glue back into the community.

Congregational caring groups (cells) and communications networks should be established so that all Christians have effective support groups. It can be seen that a church will have several systems of pastoral teams – professional and lay – overlapping each other so that individuals may participate in several of them.

Pastoral caring: We may apply this to the subject of pastoral caring. Pastors everywhere are expected to watch over their flocks and 'care' for them. ('Care' may be defined as temporary keeping until claimed by the owner.) Pastors care for people until they are claimed by the owner – God. In the urban church the range of need is so great that the pastor must limit his personal case load and rely on others. Counselling is the Church's growth industry because people need personal affirmation and help in making awesome choices and in understanding what is happening to them. This growth of counselling may be seen as the contextualising of problems in a social situation which seems out of control. Urban pastors soon realise that a counselling model centred on the client's internal problems underestimates the impact of the environment on them.

Many urban pastors over-extend themselves in personal counselling and do what congregational and family networks should do. The pastor of a low-budget church should build networks of peer professionals in law, geriatrics, medicine, education, and other areas. These can help rescue people in emergencies, and pastors should see that these caring systems and resource people are in place to be called upon in time of need. The frequency of crises among church families in cities will debilitate the hardest, most spiritually dedicated pastors if they have not established caring systems. Caring is too important to be left to the charisma or competence of paid staff members. Systems of care need careful planning and thoughtful training and networking within the congregation and community. The 'carers' themselves need effective support structures as much as the pastor, if they are not to burn-out.

Maintaining meaning

It is always as well to know the enormity of our difficulties if we are to have any hope of surviving them. I turn now to some of the ways a pastor can keep fresh, useful and vigorous.

Urban pastors survive and grow if they have a meanings system or world view which gives them assurance of their worth to the Kingdoms of God even when the city is deteriorating, and the church smaller and in worse shape than when they began. I really thought about this when I was in court for a whole day accompanying a woman who was getting divorced. I had already buried her son when he killed himself playing roulette with a gun; he spun the chamber and simply blew his head off. How could I cope with the oppression of these incidents and understand their global and Kingdom significance? Yet the woman wanted me there to support her; she turned instinctively to the church for help, because she trusted in God's caring through his people. I saw in that woman's life, suffering and faith the signs of the Kingdom, and I felt a great sense of renewal.

Pastors attempt to get meaning into their work by moving, getting additional degrees, taking leave of absence, starting some new system of personal study or initiating new programmes or missions. These may all be valid and useful at various stages in your ministry, but they are not substitutes for this essential search for global and theological significance in the trivia of daily life.

One of the purposes of this book is to indicate something of the big corporate picture within which your personal ministry is situated. To see urbanisation in global or national terms may help to produce the meanings system so necessary to keep you alive in the city. As cities get bigger, your impact on them diminishes, and you cannot compensate for your growing sense of futility by hard work and creativity alone.

You need, then, to maintain your learning. No one can ever know enough to be an urban pastor, and you learn through disciplined study, and also through honesty about your limitations – so that other people can teach you, from their very different experience and culture, how you are to be their pastor. It can be helpful to maintain one specialist area of study, to give you satisfaction from doing one thing well. Cities are very rich in learning possibilities, both formal and informal. There is no excuse for becoming stifled and intellectually bankrupt; you must take on responsibility for learning and make it a structured priority. You cannot blame the continuous urban crisis (or some other villain) for your failure to retreat, reflect and retool yourself.

Learning may come equally from your colleagues and members, and from the pluralism of your neighbours, even though the mental challenge may be different from that of a middle-class church filled with social leaders. You are receiving a global education and acquiring a global view. Christian pastors who detach themselves from the upward-mobility reward system for long enough may find the vocational equivalent of the 'born again' experience!

The pastor may also retain vision by having comparative and historical understanding. In Chapter 4 we saw Moses, Nehemiah and others living out their ministries in circumstances much more difficult than any of ours. No pastor walks alone, and maybe nothing in our era will be worse than the Black Death and the Hundred Years' War of the fourteenth century. Perhaps you think that this is too much like hitting your left hand with a hammer to make you forget how much your right hand hurts, but comparative 'fellowship' with pastors of other centuries and other places is a critical part of staying fresh and surviving.

We help to keep our vision by dreams, vision and imagination. We can falsely evaluate our work either by regarding it too pessimistically, in the light of our vision and aspirations, or by exaggerating what we have achieved. We can correct this by keeping a daily journal, as a help to objective assessment.

A personal network: Perhaps the most important of all these ways of maintaining meaning is the support of a personal network.

I was essentially a loner in ministry until I was 35 – actor, entrepreneur, programme designer and so on. In the early 1970s, I began to network with a group and realised that I was not a messiah. We call ourselves the Chicago Network and this is one of my most vital ways of staying alive in the city. In large cities all over the United States, small support groups of persons from different denominations, but highly committed to each other, emerged at this time.

Historical reflection will probably label these groups as normal responses to the programmatic activism of the sixties, but they are experienced by numbers of urban pastors as a surprising gift of grace for renewal. It took us several years to build our personal and support group because each person added changed the dynamics and the agenda. We built the group slowly and committed ourselves to making a spiritual and personal journey together. The group of 10 has now been meeting for a full day a month for a decade. We covenant annually to remain in the group, or to leave, and arrange all our dates in advance. Half of the meeting time is spent in worship, personal sharing and prayer for each other. If someone comes in real pain, we change our agenda and deal with that. When one of our former members was having difficulty at work, we went to his office unannounced and laid hands on him and prayed for him. This was a gesture to let him know that he was being supported in his difficulties. We try to have a pastoral role among the clergy of the city, and if we hear of a minister in trouble we will arrange to see him and pray for him.

The support group contains people of a variety of backgrounds and denominations, and includes Claudia Marie Barbour, the founder of Shalom Ministries in Chicago; Janet Malone who runs TRUST (To Reshape Urban Systems Together); and Hal Edwards who organises the Christian Laity of Chicago and works with the rich and influential North Shore group. Claudia Marie is a Presbyterian minister who teaches at the Catholic Theological Union and lives with a small group of nuns. Christian Laity study Jung as well as Jesus and are a network in themselves. Two of our members attend regular sessions on spiritual direction with a group of nuns – a challenge for Protestant evangelicals.

The group allows me to broaden and read things which I otherwise would not. It is easier to live in the past as an academic historian, and it is good for me that this group's emphasis is existential.

A personal support group can help all Christian pastors and leaders. A small group, highly committed to each other, can offer wider perspectives, dream new dreams and help with pain or problems. Some Christians can be renewed only within the sustained support of a Christian community. The Church as the Body of Christ and the family of God needs to see that it contains support patterns for all its members.

It is clear, then, that the urban pastor cannot stand alone; other people are necessary to him – not just networks for power and influence, but also for support and shared ministry. Once we have those other people, prepared to be co-workers, we need to examine what we are co-workers in. We need to establish our aims and methods; in short, how we will work together to be an effective urban church.

7
Worship, Work and Witness

Aims and methods for an urban church

Getting the model right

To be effective, we must have a clear idea of our aims in our urban ministry – the people we want to reach and the ways we will try to reach them.

Types of churches

We carry many biblical pictures or images of the church in our head, to communicate what churches are or should be. As a preliminary exercise, it is enjoyable and instructive for groups of Christians to decide which images most fit their churches.

Church models are the products of human culture and history, and all kinds are likely to be found in large cities. Unfortunately, pastors within these traditional models seldom encounter or enrich each other. 'Liberal' pastors may feel that they cannot develop personal relationships with 'conservative' pastors, but these categories are not the basis of this discussion. We must distinguish between cultural and theological conservatism. If a pastor discovers that he has much in common with others in very different traditions, he opens up new possibilities of effectiveness in his ministry.

My experience in Columbia, South Carolina – a city of 300,000 – showed that the churches were packaging religious experience, and the people moved from church to church as their perceived needs changed. The old idea of a church for life had gone. The young couple goes to whatever church serves its present needs. Then the wife discovers feminism and looks for a church which is not chauvinistic. Then they have a child, and look for a church with a good programme for children. The child grows up, so they need a church with a strong youth programme. By the time they're on their own again, or have divorced, they need a support ministry.

The free churches began as protests against the parish churches and therefore attracted people of a common interest from the beginning. In our highly mobile Western societies specialisation has led to fragmentation of the Christian Church into its various peer-groups, who pass each other commuting to their churches on the opposite sides of the city.

Some leaders may fear to tell urban Christians about the diversity and complexity of urban churches. They are implicitly assuming that people must be protected from doubts about the validity of their own historical model, or they will be spiritually or psychologically harmed.

Ministry and models need to be as vast, diverse and as open to change and renewal as the Church itself: the whole Gospel to the whole city. Because the city is so pluralistic, we need every single denomination, ministry-style and model. One is not better than the other, any more than a bus is better than a car. It depends upon the task to be done. There is some ministry which a house church can do, and others which a cathedral can do. Our task is not to make one like the other but to use all the models as gifts and resources for urban evangelism. Just as the general restaurant or store gives way to specialised services in the city, so the churches have had to specialise. People grow, change, and choose, and urban neighbourhoods often change very rapidly. New and specialised ministries appear at such times of necessity, next door to our church buildings or within them.

Special congregations: We will first consider churches by the needs of people attracted to them.

Many blue-collar workers and minority groups are looking for an authoritarian pulpit figure. In the factory they may be shouted at and ordered about, and every Sunday they go to church and get verbally spanked. It hurts, but they come out feeling good. At least they are relating to someone they feel cares.

A growing class of churches attract event-centred, 'now oriented' people – the sort who read the church page on

Saturday to see where God will be on Sunday. There is a great hunger for celebration in the city, and these people are reached by liturgical renewal – and they are fuelling the charismatic renewal. They will drive 40 miles to sit anonymously and clap hands and sing for joy. They will praise God and hug people they do not even know.

Another group are people who want relationships. They are turned off by anonymous charismatic celebration. Their lives have been fragmented by the city; their extended families are scattered across town, or back in the home village or even the home country. Their needs are met by the church as a small group, often meeting in a house. These churches do not grow, but their numbers grow. House churches are proliferating and act as support groups and families for their members. These folk are hungering for a community, and preferably one which does not change.

Then there are the task-oriented, active people who are attracted to churches with extensive programmes which demand high commitment – lawyers, doctors, young professional people of all kinds. A general distinction can be made between people who want to be and those who want to do. If a church is to be successful it needs both kinds of people represented on all its committees.

Specialised churches: In the turbulent environment of cities, human needs become exaggerated, and growing churches often specialise in one of these approaches. People will be drawn to or repulsed by the various models of ministry according to their own personalities. Pastors often experience this as personal rejection but it is not.

To meet all these varying needs there are several common types of church.

A *cathedral* is the highly visible and symbolic centre of church authority. Its theological starting point may be the Lordship and transcendence of Christ over all his creation, including the business and politics of the city. Its godly members assume with Calvin that they can minister vocationally in their factories and businesses, even viewing their work as acts of praise and worship.

Immigrant and ex-ethnic churches include the first-generation churches with imported language, customs and symbols; and also churches who after three or four generations still retain some cultural feel for the 'old country' even though they no longer use its language. The 'old country' ethos usually remains long after the congregation has adopted the vernacular and accepted non-ethnic members.

House churches are a New Testament model; they may take many forms, from cells in parishes to informal groups. House churches suit people who are looking for reality and integrity in their personal relationships. They have a strong body-life and are without strong professional leadership. Because of this they may suit middle-class communities better than poor ones, as the very poor lack confidence and need structures and buildings around which to relate.

International churches serve temporary expatriate communities.

Multi-language churches feature several different language groups meeting separately in one building.

Parish churches are European models, and function as chaplains to their neighbourhoods as well as to their congregation. Historically, the Church of England vicar is given the 'cure of souls' of his entire parish.

Sectarian churches usually have some unusual or bizarre beliefs or behaviour; they usually consist of urban people who feel excluded socially and theologically.

Super-churches are highly organised, independent, with multiple programmes. They have strong, usually authoritarian leadership, and a compulsive mission desire to grow and reach as many people as possible.

Task churches organise varied and sophisticated urban projects and attract activist believers with strong commitment. They express their faith politically, socially and liturgically.

The structure of churches

While you are analysing what type your church is, there is another aspect worth consideration: the balance of power and action within the church – what we may call the church structure.

Dr Bill Leslie, pastor of La Salle Street Church, Chicago, talks about the 'athletic' church structure, where pastors and staff perform and the people watch and boo, hiss, clap or cheer. Church becomes like the definition of football, 'where 50,000 people who desperately need exercise watch 22 people who desperately need rest'. The pastor's role should be to mobilise the gifts of the whole church, not to perform for them, however brilliantly or tirelessly.

A second athletic image might be that of the most successful college basketball coach in all history, John Wooden of California. He began with short, fast, mostly white players, and won his first national championship with that team. Some years later he ended up with mostly black and very tall players, but he was still winning; he kept changing his system of offensive and defensive patterns to fit the material of his team. We all know coaches (and pastors) who do just the opposite, of course. They struggle to make the players fit their system, and ignore any great talent that does not fit their rigid idea of what a team (or a church) ought to look like.

The fortress model: The traditional church is too often of the 'athletic' variety and has a 'come-all-ye' structure in which people must be brought into the church programmes in order to find Christ. They are then discipled into the covenant fellowship and incorporated into the lifestyle of the church. Growth expands the centre, and incorporation into the congregation is assumed as the goal of discipleship. Church growth is measured at the centre as the programmes expand, buildings are developed and budgets increase. This pattern has become the norm for church life in the USA, and recent literature on ministry roles generally assumes its validity.

The 'come-all-ye' structure expects everything important to take place at the centre around the pulpit and programmes. It is a busy and well-organised church. Its strength is that it provides security and structure for people. Given the insecurity of our time, this model, with a strong, charismatic and often authoritarian pastor, can achieve a great deal of visible success in the city. People who usually feel insignificant can feel strong in this church. It provides psychological importance, marshalls resources in task directions, and assimilates people into programmes. It is the 'fortress model' of the church.

The expeditionary-force model: The 'go' system – or the expeditionary-force model – regards the church members as ministers to their worlds of relationships. Earlier I showed how Beverley and Mary-Ann did this at Fairfield Avenue Baptist Church. In the 'come-all-ye' system a banker, for example, might teach Sunday School and serve on the church finance committee. He would experience the corporate programme of the church as a vicarious ministry. In the 'go' model the same banker would identify a mission within the bank, perhaps running a Bible study with his colleagues or even planning resources to help build up neglected neighbourhoods.

The 'go' model offers advantages for an urban church: firstly because it legitimises the call to lay mission; secondly because it reaches more widely and follows the urban 24-hour clock, something no church can really do with its programmes; and thirdly because it fulfils the need of specialised urban people to affirm their personal vocations as their ministry. In this model the pastoral task is to help these members identify, plan for and equip themselves for their diverse ministry opportunities.

No church would wish to be a 'come-all-ye' or 'go' as a pure type, but could aim at being a mixture of both. The healthy church is a dynamic combination of the two. However, my experiences and conversations in many cities of the world suggest that most pastors would need immense mental transformations to allow the second model to work. This is partly because the pastoral task is so huge and diffuse, and as a result pastors tend to structure their ministries in ways they can control.

The multiracial challenge

In this increasingly interconnected planet where the mission is now on all continents, the churches at home must begin to model with integrity that which they have sent missionaries abroad to do. By sending them abroad in the first place, the

Church was confessing a trans-cultural commitment to the oneness of Jesus Christ. Urban pastors must practise it. Certainly there are skills required, but as in so many other areas, the key to handling urban diversity is not primarily a set of skills, but a perspective on what God has been doing and continues to do in the world.

Language, faith and race

Today many urban communities are migrant centres. Those of us who approach them as outsiders may have strong convictions that these people should convert to follow Jesus, and therefore assimilate into the cultural values, structures, congregations and communities we create for them. This is a short-sighted view. Immigrants can eventually enrich us all in the city, but those pastors and churches that reach out ought to study the newcomers' culture, history and if possible their languages before expecting them to follow Jesus. While a few individuals may immediately convert and assimilate, it may be at great psychological or spiritual cost to their families later.

Teaching a culture: Jane Addams and Julia Lathrop left their wealthy Rockford homes in 1889, and moved into a large house in the midst of Chicago's worst West Side slum. There they confronted the 'masses' – those Italian, Greek Orthodox and Polish Catholic immigrants who flooded into Chicago. The fashionable lakefront establishment feared these people whom they regarded as papists and scum. Laws and policies were directed against them with such vengeance that the people were driven deeper into their own languages, politics and churches, as a way of surviving in the city.

Jane Addams, a graduate of Rockford Women's Seminary (a young ladies' finishing school), loved the Greek language and the Greek classics because of her seminary training. When she moved in next door to the Greeks of Chicago, she saw crime, ignorance, disease and prejudice at first hand. She lived with it. Her approach to the Greeks is instructive for pastors in multi-ethnic communities today. Because the Ottoman Turks had ruled Greece for centuries and badly treated its peoples, the Greeks of Chicago did not really know what it meant to be Greek. Jane Addams founded the first Greek theatre in the United States that actually used Greeks as actors, and she taught Greek to Greeks as part of her ministry among them.

Addams' way of approaching immigrants or migrants was fundamentally sound. She knew that before people can integrate into a church or society they must have a sense of identity and a sense of security, and she helped the poor Greek immigrants to find both. Her treatment of Greeks was rooted in a profound respect for their culture, and the ability to use their languages.

Making relationships: My second example is a Christian businessman whom I recently visited in Surabaya, Indonesia, and his ministry illustrates the principle of approaching people strongly committed to another religion. This Pentecostal businessman left his job and took his family to an appalling slum – almost a garbage dump. The area was filling up with devout Muslims from Madura, and the businessman built his house out of crates like everyone else. He began by asking his well-off friends for donations, and then called the men of the community together and said, 'My Christian friends want you to have this money to build your mosque.' He then spent six months helping them to build the mosque. He began a Bible-study with the people with whom he worked, and eventually 30 adult believers had been baptised, with 30 teenagers coming to afternoon classes.

Most mission boards would recall that man for his actions, but this is just the sort of radical, upside-down perspective that we need. This kind of tough love is not supported by most churches and missions. I learned from this amazing example that dialogue with Islam must take place in love and never out of defensiveness, apologetics or militant evangelism. We have not invested in making relationships like this; we are depriving the thousands who are left unsatisfied by Islam of the chance to experience our Good News.

Recognising racism: Racism is still a widespread sin in our churches, and we need to identify it and deal with it. Here is an honest testimony by a Christian woman in London.

> I settled in the main Bangladeshi part of London and I had to confront – firstly – the racism of other people in my church, and then – more painfully – my own racism. I went to Pakistan with a very traditional missionary society and was taught to identify with local people, learn their customs and language and live sacrificially because the people were poor. The white missionaries assumed that because they had come from a 'Christian' country, they knew all the answers, and were superior to the local people. I was never happy with this attitude but never challenged it, and I lived with this system for nearly six years. Even after my return I had still not identified this problem as racism. I knew that it was to do with rich and poor and about power, but I had not realised that white society was riddled with racism. In my church many people hated the Bangladeshis, or at least wished they were not there. If they had all packed up and left, the church people would have been delighted. I felt that there was no Good News for the Bangladeshis when Christians hated them, or wanted them to go.
>
> The Lord then showed me my own racism. I had grown to accept and love the Bangladeshis, but I still accepted as normal that all the people who collected the tickets or swept the roads were black; that the people who did the most inferior or menial jobs were black; and that they had inferior housing and higher-than-average rates of unemployment. If as Christians we are members of the Kingdom of God in which all women and men are valued and can reach their true humanity, whatever their race and background, then in our churches we need to find practical ways of living this out.

Let a black student from my own seminary describe his

experience of racism.

> When I entered kindergarten – a fine Catholic school – I realised that I was the only black person in the class. I sensed that people looked at me, and I found that I had other names like 'nigger' and 'spear-chucker', all these extra nouns by which my mother and father had never referred to me. What does it mean to be in a place where you do not seem to be wanted? What does it mean to look in newspapers and magazines and Sunday School books and not see any illustrations that refer to you? Reading the history of America, it seems that black people did not play a part in it at all. If you could stand up to the prejudice, to the oppression and to the knowledge that you were hated, then you were somebody because only somebody can do that. To be black in the United States is to have pride and dignity – if you can call it that – because you have been able to survive. You don't have to be in America to be hated because you are black; you can be hated right here in London too. These people do not even know you, but they hate you. People who are being oppressed themselves also hate you. They have no feelings of compassion, of brotherhood, of love, in the sense of coming together to make things better for the brotherhood of all mankind. Being black in the United States is no bad thing because God has used us to do a great job. God has used the black people to demonstrate his hand in mankind.

These accounts indicate to us that urban churches must develop their thinking and strategies about their multi-ethnic communities if they are to be effective and honour their Lord. The institutional church in a formerly stable parish is usually ill-equipped to face immigration, and its congregation seldom responds willingly or easily to the new realities. These churches may have had a foreign mission emphasis – 'over there, somewhere'. Host churches seem to have forgotten the virtue of hospitality. Christians need not trivialise or paternalise uprooted peoples by supposing that their immediate needs (food, shelter, employment or medical care) are their deepest needs; nor lump them into stereotypes; nor avoid personal involvement with them. Migrants may be driven into social isolation and be invisible though next door to us. Others are forced to leave, or to assimilate into existing communities.

Other faiths and other Christians: I have given a telling example of a Christian leader relating to another religion, but I am disturbed about Islam. It is held to be the perfect urban faith, because it seems to control people. In Chicago two-thirds of all grocery stores are owned by Arabs, there are 34 mosques, and Islam is growing very rapidly. I think we will be seeing some religious conflict in our cities, probably even in London. I will not be happy if we solve our racial conflicts and then revert to religious ones. Religious differences occur not only in Beirut, but everywhere, from Colombo, Sri Lanka, to Belfast.

One can easily understand the difficulties of relating to those of other faiths; it is harder to see why our churches have equal difficulty in respecting and understanding the histories and diversities of migrants from Christian traditions. We should reach out in love to everyone, but especially to our Christian brothers. Yet often, Christian churches have been ostracised by the Christian community because they house people of another culture.

An example is the black churches of America. Because of discrimination, they have often had to develop a wide variety of enterprises, and the black pastors developed great leadership skills because the black churches became places with all kinds of social and caring networks. In London many black churches are not autonomous, but off-shoots of American denominations. Often these have their headquarters in the American Bible belt, and then local ecumenical co-operation is discouraged, and they are restricted from forming relationships with mainstream churches. There is still a debate in the black churches in Britain about whether they should get involved in social, economic and political issues at all. Many regard these as diversions from the spiritual and personal emphases which are characteristic of their faith.

How to be multicultural

It may be helpful now to define 'culture' before going on to list some practical principles by which urban churches might effect multicultural ministries. Here are some criteria for defining cultural boundaries:

Common place of origin
Race
Language or dialect
Religious faith
Shared traditions, values and symbols
Literature, folklore and music
Food preferences
Settlement and employment patterns
Special political interests in the homeland or present home country
Special institutions
Feelings of being distinctive.

The forms in which these integrated beliefs are expressed are dynamic. Cities are like zoos to which our reaction may be a mixture of awe at the existence of so many glorious and inglorious creatures in God's creation, and sadness at seeing them in so confined an urban environment, in which the splendour of so many rural cultures is brutally beaten down. Culture is a gift to people. It provides identity and security in the city and opportunity for the Church. But when so many different cultural groups enter a common geographical space, how shall we respond to the challenge?

For many urban pastors the struggle with ethnic and linguistic diversity is not easy, and with increasing frequency one hears them refer to the 'homogeneous unit principle' as a reason to resegregate the churches under the guise of growth. The theory that the churches which grow fastest are monocultural is widely accepted in the church growth movement. I must reject this thinking as incompatible with biblical teaching, and offer these practical ideas for developing a multicultural Christian witness.

Have a vision: Both host and migrant believers need affirmation for their special roles in God's task of world-wide evangelism. Host Christians may recognise that many of the most culturally distant new refugees have values much closer to biblical norms for behaviour and family life than those of many resident Christians. Do not take narrow, traditional views of your role and responsibilities, or blame the victims for what has happened to them.

Study the culture and history of the migrants: There are good sources in many languages and your study should include the history of the group in your city. Most large cities have historical societies and the universities have their libraries and urban sociology departments. Books and experiences will help you to be sensitive to the hungers and aspirations of the various peoples around you.

Visit the various ethnic groups: Do this whether or not they are Christian. Listen to the stories of your neighbours from other countries, and try to understand their origins, and the experiences which make them unique. These visits should involve both pastors and members. You can contact migrant groups by helping their service organisations, or by founding such organisations where they are needed and do not already exist. Provide space in church for support services.

Share your faith with churches of other ethnic groups: Pastors and members love to walk you through the art, architecture, theology and history of their people. Some Christians come from churches founded by missionaries; others have found Christ in refugee camps because the Gospel was faithfully and ingeniously proclaimed there; and others come from ancient Near-Eastern churches overlaid with centuries of cultural tradition which has survived persecution in a hostile environment. Some of these stories should be shared with the whole congregation. Few things are so spiritually satisfying as the personal discoveries of Christians that their faith transcends national identities or languages, and that the blood of Jesus Christ atones for sin across all human barriers like geography, language, race or class.

It is the responsibility of the host churches to make contact, and then affirm and enable the new churches to do their evangelistic task in ways that use their unique gifts. One possible result might be the renewal of host churches in partnership with churches of other ethnic groups, directly for mission and evangelism. Those groups were linked only symbolically before, by missionaries who alone experienced the big picture and mediated between the local and distant believers. Now congregations are experiencing these relationships directly.

Develop local multilingual leadership: You may have to struggle to gain access to the resources of the international mission boards, or set aside Christians to learn a second language. In Fairfield Avenue Baptist Church, for example, we had services in Russian, Spanish, Polish, Blacktalk and English.

Visit schools: Schools must cope with diversity because they cannot relocate. Schoolteachers have developed multicultural relationships much more than church leaders, and urban port-of-entry head teachers are aware of their importance in the international streams of migrants. Wise head teachers begin where the students are, and put a great deal of effort into developing a climate of acceptability and security in the building. They also motivate their staffs to affirm cultural diversity. You should visit your local schools, but also 'model' schools which are laboratories of learning about this issue.

Pastors can learn to care for people in a migrant stream, and congregations can accept far more diversity than they have known in the past – just as urban teenagers have done in the schools. We live in a racially divided world, and bringing Kingdom peace among cultures must be an important sign of the Spirit's work.

The Church's mission

Ministry flows from the heart of the believer towards God in worship; towards other believers in fellowship and nurture; and towards the world in evangelism and social action. Mission includes everything God's Church continues to be and to do in the world, and must be rooted in the character and purpose of God, its source and sustainer. The Church's mission includes these biblically authorised tasks: worship, evangelism, discipleship, fellowship, stewardship, service.

Worship

There can be no separation of the Church's worship from work and witness, but I emphasise its priority, and its continuity with service outside the sanctuary. True communion with God can occur anywhere at any time, with other worshippers, or when one is alone, but Christian corporate worship is much more than individual communion with God. It is nothing less than continuous public dialogue between God and his people through the Word. The word 'orthodoxy' means literally 'right thinking', and the heart of our worship experience is our appropriate response to God's redemptive activity in our lives, and forms the basis of our work in, and witness to, the world.

In the New Testament the word 'liturgy' (*leitourgia*) is used very broadly. It includes:

The Old Testament Priesthood	Luke 1:5-23, Hebrews 7:21, 10:11
Jesus' ministry	Hebrews 8:2, 6
Prayer service at Antioch	Acts 13:2
The passing of offering plates	Romans 15:27
Financial support	Philippians 2:25, 30
The public service of Roman government officials	Romans 13:6

Paul also used the word 'liturgy' to describe both prominent public activity, and menial tasks such as sweeping out the forum in preparation for meetings. 'Liturgy', then, is a word for ministry – although not the only one in the Bible – and defines a much broader and more significant activity than we generally suppose, ranging from the activity of Jesus, to prayer and public service. 'Ministry' in the Bible includes worship, work and witness. Worship has the pastoral priority in the life of the healthy and effective church.

When new Christians are born into Christ's Body (I Cor. 12:13), they are built together (I Pet. 2:5ff), and given identity and meaning. Their relationships with God, their families and their environment are all new. God graciously forgives and liberates sinners and then welcomes them into his presence as family members. Healing and communication take place during worship. Within God's family there need be no apology for viewing worship as an end in itself, not as a means to achieve other goals in the Church whose chief end is to 'glorify God and enjoy him for ever'. Worship is that which we owe to God because the Church is his. In our congregational worship services we rehearse the drama of our salvation in words and actions. The parts in the drama are taken by God's people and the pastor and the other enablers are the prompters. The Lord God himself is the appreciative audience.

Designing worship: The functions of worship are common to all congregations, but each will vary the forms of worship to suit its unique history, personality and culture. What enables a congregation to worship meaningfully in one context may be a barrier to it in another. How would you design worship for the congregation described below?

There are new adult Christians who have not been to churches or Sunday Schools before.

The families prefer to keep their children with them during the services rather than separate them in crêches or Sunday Schools.

There are people of different languages and cultures who wish to hear their own styles of music and speech for at least part of the service.

There are poor people who are told what to do by institutions and individuals all week long.

There are people who are experiencing increasingly difficult times with little or no hope of improvement.

The principles upon which you would design the worship arise from these criteria and you should develop a list for your own congregation. They might be:

We shall use a simple translation of the Bible and always give the page numbers in the bulletin and during the service.

We shall make the services relevant to people whose attention spans are short and whose vocabularies are limited.

Our worship-leaders and ushers will reflect the different cultural groups, and we will use their languages and types of music.

During the services our poor people will be given time and encouragement to talk back to God and other members in the church.

We shall celebrate our lives and find meaning for them in our worship.

We shall make entry into the congregation as easy as possible for the community. (People are often so offended by our thoughtless worship forms that they never have a real opportunity to be offended by the Cross.)

The service begins with a call to worship in a variety of ways and by a variety of people. Then the congregation approaches God and hears him through his Word. The second part includes times of giving, sharing and praying for one another. Decisions, commitments, challenges and concerns are shared, and people can respond to the sermon – perhaps in ways the preacher did not expect. Worship is followed by instruction and fellowship in small groups.

Some Christians view the worship service as a retreat from the turbulent present into the nostalgia of an imagined past, but this view is not adequate. The service must provide shelter and acceptance to disturbed and bewildered people without being merely a crutch to lean on, or a narcotic which offers only temporary compensation and not reality.

Preaching

Preaching is a major part of worship and the development of the congregation. I suggested earlier that pastors need to stimulate people to look back on past events and achievements, and that this will increase their capacity to plan for the future. It may take several years for a congregation to develop a healthy approach to experience: able to utilise their memories of the past and look forward to the future with confidence. Congregations need to know that they are the redeemed people of God and have roots and identity. New pastors need not attempt to change church institutions. Congregations will adapt these themselves to suit the new awareness developed by the preaching.

We can use the example of Israel's ancient festivals. They were aware that God was redeeming them in history, and so reflected on their special events and enshrined them in calendars and liturgies. Three well-known examples are the deliverance from Egypt (Passover), provision in the wilderness (Tabernacles), and deliverance in Persia (Purim). Urban congregations identify with Israel's pilgrimage, and good preaching needs to explain the historical context of the events, so that the hearers can make connections with their own situation and experience. The Psalms – the Hebrew song book – did not fall down out of the sky after all!

The congregation can be helped to develop its own 'feast cycle' if it understands the background of the biblical events, and monthly, seasonal and annual events can be planned with drama, art, music, and especially stories of how God has been and is at work.

Using scripture: Many church pastors use printed lectionaries, and these have advantages. The pastor is forced to study passages in which he may have little interest. Pastors who preach on whatever they want get lazy and miss the meanings of large parts of scripture. At least one day a week, or its equivalent, is needed for the sermon even for a busy, crisis-oriented pastor, and involves regular, well planned, long-term scripture study and a related reading programme.

The challenge of preaching is increased by the diversity of levels and languages demanded: Jesus used stories, and so may the urban preacher. Much of scripture is in story form and people respond to stories. There are different types of literature in the Bible, and the right way to preach them flows from the text itself. Prepare the sermon first to speak to your personal needs, and then wrestle with the way to communicate that message to your diverse audience.

Develop and communicate a contagious love for scripture since the Holy Spirit promises to bless that to the hearers. A great theme verse for preachers and teachers is John 14:26, where Jesus makes two wonderful promises. Firstly, the Spirit would help the disciples remember what he had said. They sometimes slept through his messages! Secondly, the Spirit would lead them into new truth which Jesus had not had the opportunity to share with them. Fortunately, the Spirit still does both these things for us.

Good preaching and liturgy meet many needs, and funerals and weddings can provide opportunities for care and support. Churches need thoughtful, well-established procedures for these major public rites, so that the newest or the poorest members understand their theological significance. These procedures are best worked out corporately – perhaps through the worship committee – and designed to show that the pastor is not the only caring person in the church.

Evangelism

I part company with those who say, 'Only do a social ministry,' and with those who say, 'We only announce the Good News.' It is the News which transforms the climate and gives people hope. Only then can they find the energy to change things. The way some good news was received in a German prisoner-of-war camp illustrates this principle. Murdo McDonald spoke to his American colleagues through the fence in Gaelic, because English was not permitted. In 1945 they exchanged the news that the war was over – three days before the Germans heard it. During these three days they were still prisoners of war, with all the accustomed privations. Nothing had changed. But before the gates had been unlocked the good news had transformed their response to their situation. This is a parable of the way the Gospel can transform the lives of people who often remain in unemployment, poverty and other types of urban oppression.

The Gospel is news, not advice. The difference between

Jesus Christ and the newspaper problem page is just at this point. Good advice is something to do, whether it be to repent, feel guilty, or whatever. I cannot go into the ghetto with integrity and tell people that they are bad and need to change, or to feel more guilty than they do. Jesus forgave people first. He did not ignore sin and he had a profound understanding of it, but he did not go to poor people and lay guilt and the law on them.

Christians cannot work in poor urban areas and not offer the Good News. If they do social work and all kinds of things and have failed to offer the Good News, they have failed to offer their best gift. Jesus offers something he has already done for you. Urban pastors like Peter and John in Acts 3 may have had few resources, but they always had News. There is no excuse for not sharing that News with all people every day, and in clear ways that give people the opportunity to accept or reject Jesus. How can we say we truly care for people if we do not care enough to confront them unambiguously with who Jesus Christ is and what he can do for them? Surely Carl Henry was right when he said, 'All ways of not evangelising are always wrong.' The late Paul Little was fond of saying, 'Scratch people where they itch in the name of Jesus Christ.' Caring about someone's personal needs is part of evangelism.

Impersonal evangelism: In my evangelism classes I use the Lausanne Covenant definition, that evangelism is the Good News of the Gospel about Jesus, which we proclaim by our words and our actions. The content of evangelism is who Jesus is, what he did, and what he continues to do. Jesus is the one who came into the world, lived and died and rose again, and now is the ascended, risen Lord who offers forgiveness to all who repent and believe. How then do we offer this Gospel?

Earlier I described the 'overload' upon urban people resulting from their being swamped with 'secondary', or impersonal, casual relationships. They switch off from making these relationships. In lifts or underground trains they avoid looking at each other and stare blankly. I concluded that impersonal styles of evangelism – door-knocking, media or mailing, and giant crusades – do not take urban realities into account. The electronic media and the Billy Graham style of campaigns are probably regarded by most American and British evangelists as still the ideal ways to reach cities with the Gospel. Such campaigns have valid roles but they were not the primary means used by the Early Church, nor are they the most effective means in our large, complex cities today.

Programmes for evangelism become additional layers of work for our already busy people, and are usually invitations for the public to come to our buildings. Pastors may prefer programmes for these reasons:

They have not taken the time to identify the primary lines of communication which already exist for urban dwellers.
The programmes may have been effective in their previous churches.
They were taught these styles of evangelism in college.
Their denominations expect or promote programmes.
They have budgets set aside for programmes.
Their own 'pastoral ego' requires them to be visible and productive in evangelism before their church members.

An example of inappropriate impersonal evangelism is the telephone evangelism attempted in Chicago by one Christian group. They called every number in the phone book and invited people to respond to Jesus. The programme was a disaster. It did not reach half our families, who are without telephones. Many of those with telephones did not speak English. Those who did speak English simply did not make this sort of decision on the telephone. You cannot call up an anonymous person in the city and deal with eternal issues. The method is incongruous and violates the whole psychology of urban people.

Personal evangelism: I would suggest that the only evangelism suitable in urban contexts is personal – church members ministering to their own 'worlds of relationships': family and extended family (biological); geographical; vocational. Each person draws a chart of his or her relationships in each of these worlds. The family chart includes the 'nuclear family' – the household – and the extended family, which may be scattered over the whole country. (My family, like most urban families, does not live in one locality. My parents live in Denver, Colorado, 1,000 miles from Chicago; my brother lives in Washington DC, which is 750 miles in the opposite direction.) Church members then identify a basic need for each person, and select three or four of their family networks to minister to in practical ways.

The second network – the geographical – consists of people you have a primary relationship with, or could have, by virtue of where you live. They may be your neighbours, or occupy other flats in your building. They include your barber, the person you buy your food from, the mechanic who fixes your car, and the teacher of your child. The procedure is the same: select a few of these people and identify a need for each, and think how you plan to minister to them and share Jesus with them.

The third network is vocational. In order to help people minister in their workplaces I suggest that the pastor should make his second call – if not his first – where they work. Most urban pastors know very little about their members' worlds of work, unlike their rural colleagues who know everyone's work. In the city the congregation disappears during the week and the pastor has no idea what they do. His preaching becomes barren and irrelevant and he has no idea how to illustrate it. Some urban pastors may have created alternative congregational worlds for urban people, to compensate for their own loss of reality because they know so little about the urban world.

Many pastors have an anachronistic view of work. They communicate to their people that real work is 'church work' – by which they mean loyalty to church programmes. Luther put this idea out of date when he emptied the monasteries with the rediscovery that you could serve God in your vocation. Calvin affirmed that and went further, suggesting that you could serve God with your vocation. Pastors can help members to minister within their vocations. The results will be less visible in the sanctuary, perhaps, because the members will be occupied within their own worlds with counselling, Bible studies, and a whole range of mercy ministries. Pastors will encourage maturing members to assume union or management responsibilities, and will adopt a posture of listening and learning to accomplish this. The maturing Christians must describe their worlds for us, before we can help them to get involved effectively.

The 'come-all-ye' church structure, involving people in programmes within the church, is especially ineffective with men, whose primary identity is through their work. The pastor invites them to set aside this identity and enter a world in which the pastor is high and lifted up in the pulpit, and is the chief executive officer of the 'corporation' called 'church'. It is hardly fair or effective for pastors to ask lay people to leave their worlds of vocational identity all the time, and come into the church and be a vocational non-person among other worshippers, while the pastors parade their unique identity before them. This may explain why some male ministers have difficulty in reaching men, and why women come in such abundance. The pastor may be too vocationally overpowering for other males to feel comfortable.

Pastors should deliberately enter the several worlds of their members, and listen to their personal and corporate histories. Visits to their places of work affirm their members' identities and their call to mission in their vocations, which are areas where pastors have limited access. If the whole city is to be reached, members will have to do it in each of their worlds. The pastor can visit people in their factories and offices for lunch, ask them about their work, and help them to chart and think about the people with whom they work. In my ministry our church's evangelism was transformed by these visits to people at work; my encouragement of members to regard themselves as ministers opened up most of our opportunities. All this costs nothing because it takes advantage of the networks that already exist.

It is not an addition to people's crowded church programmes like most evangelism, inviting people to meetings, or calling door-to-door. These are really tiresome activities in the city – yet more duties for busy people. A congregation of 100 active members, where people are encouraged to identify ministry in all three networks, is no small church. It is the inability to see that the field really is the world that keeps urban pastors feeling insignificant. We must remember that our pastoral goal in the city is effective ministry, not the efficiency of our programmes.

Teaching evangelism: My search has been for some simple way to enable people to share their faith – a way which fits the social realities of cities. Most fruitful evangelism comes through the primary networks of believers, so the key is to help people to identify them, and then teach them how to share their faith. People are not motivated by books on evangelism, or by your saying, 'Would you go to this conference? It will teach you how to become an evangelist.' Few lay people get excited by that. They need to be trained singly or in small groups, firstly, to give a simple testimony. This should have three parts:

My life before I met Jesus.
How I met Jesus.
The difference in my life since I met Jesus.

Then they need a few simple questions to start a conversation:

Are you interested in religion these days?
Can I take a couple of minutes and tell you what Jesus means to me?
Would you like to become a Christian?
Can I tell you how I became a Christian?

Most denominations have evangelism material in their churches, and some is superb. There is no room however for subterfuges, or 'foot-in-the-door' play for other agenda. Pastors need to develop the expectation that their church members will share the Gospel as a matter of course and in ways appropriate to their personalities, and to the time, place and audience. This is friendship evangelism – teaching lay people how to approach their friends and serve them in love.

Another training principle I recommend for pastors is

never to do anything alone. It is more efficient to make a hospital visit alone, but I went alone only in an emergency. I would take Tom with me to visit Mrs Skulsky, and on the way I would say, 'By the way, Tom, Mrs Skulsky wasn't in church on Sunday. Would you be able to tell her about the service?' Or, 'I think Mrs Skulsky would enjoy hearing your testimony; would you mind telling her how you became a believer?' In the hospital I would introduce Mrs Skulsky to Tom and ask her to introduce her friend in the next bed. The visit might include Tom's story of how he met Jesus, and prayer in which both our church member and her neighbouring patient are involved. Afterwards I would help Tom to recall and interpret the experience so that he could begin to make calls on his own. 'Tom, I think you are ready to make calls now yourself. And you know something? They expect me to make calls because they pay me, but when you come to the hospital they are really excited because they know you must care. Nobody expects lay people to come.'

In these ways your people will become evangelistic and they will draw upon their pastor for follow-on, or help with problems as they arise. Encourage your people to share testimonies – not 'bragimonies' – that illustrate who Jesus is and what he does. Conversion has been described as a radical act. Set people free from sin's awful bondage, and you may start an urban social revolution.

Discipleship and fellowship

Discipleship is serving Jesus as Lord. I have given the example of our Christians in Action groups at Fairfield Baptist Church, and other aspects of discipleship may be considered under the headings of evangelism, stewardship and service.

Fellowship is the community dimension of congregational life, so gloriously present in the book of Acts, and so painfully absent in so many of our Western churches. Western living scatters families across continents, and abandons the elderly, the sick and the poor. Huge and growing populations of socially marginal people seek shelter in the cities because they alone retain the public services. The urban church must function intentionally as a community and as a family for these people, through caring teams, housegroups, cells, and ministries to people in crisis, and to the elderly. That is, ministries of or by the elderly, poor and needy are required, rather than ministries to them. Some outside resources are helpful, but professional staff should see their work as engaging and empowering people to help themselves and each other.

Many evangelicals fail to understand how urban people satisfy their need for fellowship. Neighbourhood bars, pubs, clubs or bingo-sessions are crowded and noisy – and consolatory. These scenes might assault the senses of church deacons and elders, or the middle-class, highly educated congregations, but they tell a lot about the social needs and fellowship styles of the urban people we often find hard to reach.

Love for each other across racial and class barriers still remains the most powerful testimony to Jesus Christ and the Gospel. The local church must demonstrate fellowship to communities turfed by gangs, divided by political corruption and ruined by financial exploitation.

A new and loving acceptance can be communicated through street parties, music groups, backyard picnics and street art and drama. Demonstrate community and fellowship as well as preach it, and the people will gladly hear the Gospel in your sermons.

Stewardship and service

Stewardship is obviously much more than tithing. We are stewards of minds, bodies, abilities, time, place and relationships. Christians have new identities which lead to new tasks, release energy, and radically change perspectives. 'Once you were not a people, but now you are the people of God; once you had not received mercy, but now you have received mercy' (1 Pet. 2:10). New values shape every area of life and change people culturally and socially. They may formerly have cared only for themselves and their family, but now they are concerned for their neighbourhood, schools, the poor and indeed the entire city. A Christian behaves as a steward when he or she works towards the renewal of urban social systems – for health, education, transport, justice, housing and sanitation – because God is concerned for the health and fairness of these systems. Our stewardship is far more significant than most people realise, and our preaching and action must show this. Stewardship is closely related to service and leads to activity.

Service in action: In our cities we have increasing numbers of old, isolated people, living on fixed incomes which are devalued constantly by inflation. They are forced in the winter to choose between food and fuel. Many starve, and many freeze to death each year in Chicago. We now need churches in our Western cities which have special ministries to – and of – senior citizens. Many American churches are now employing Senior Citizens' co-ordinators with networks around them.

Churches also need to rethink their entire youth ministries, especially in cities with millions of young children, and where children increasingly live only with their mothers.

The church may become involved in relief of all kinds of need. I know a Christian in Calcutta who made little stickers saying, 'If you have trouble, please phone . . .' and stuck them on walls and telephone boxes. He then trained 16 volunteer women to answer the phone in shifts. Many people responded: people so ashamed, bitter or alienated that they could talk only anonymously on the phone. That ministry has led to Samaritan work, a strong church, and a half-way programme for drug addicts.

Another ministry in Caracas advertised telephone counselling using five answerphones. The recorded message gave a 30-second description of the service and invited the caller to leave his name and telephone number. The founder began to get more calls than he could handle, and so trained others to do the counselling, working round the clock. This ministry led to a new church which meets in a theatre. It currently has 300 members.

A Catholic business woman in Manila bought cheap air time at night to provide TV for insomniacs. She studied people who could not sleep and found that they shared a group of common problems. On her show she has people talking about these problems and offering a telephone number, so that during the transmission calls are coming in and being followed up by counselling. Rich and poor, hurting people, victims of crime and injustice, the bereaved and distressed are being reached at night.

Church members in Bangkok began to work with mentally handicapped children in their community and started a little school. They discovered thousands of physically and mentally handicapped children; with other evangelical churches they formed an alliance to persuade the government to accept some responsibility for the children's education.

In Chicago a group of Christians moved into a red-light district and became involved with a network of prostitutes and pimps. They were unable to release the women from prostitution without offering alternative sources of income. Many were mothers, and the Christians began by baby-sitting while they were soliciting. Their ministry developed into legal work to release the women from contractual obligations with their pimps; job-finding; and fighting the landlords and politicians who owned the buildings used for prostitution and who profited by it. The Christians had to develop a political and legal strategy to deal with this reality.

The lesson from these examples is that we must be prepared to go on for a long time and get involved in all kinds of issues. We need to work in very practical ways, and I do not know many churches prepared to do that.

From relief to reform: These Christians moved from relief to reform: action includes both. Your refusal to act is a powerful political action which supports the status quo. When Paul asked Philemon to receive Onesimus, he contravened Roman law, which demanded that a runaway slave be branded or executed. Philemon's acceptance of Onesimus was a social act which fleshed out what Paul had said earlier, that there is no difference between slave or free. Jesus' healing of the blind and those with leprosy must be seen as a social act, and not just as 'signs and wonders' which need not be copied by us.

The Early Church did not have access to the political power

possessed by modern Christians, and we cannot stay neutral. Christians who refuse to pay part of their taxes in protest at what they regard as excessive military expenditure, are demonstrating their Christian consciences.

A black politician in London – Paul Boateng – told a consultation at which I was present,

> Christians in Europe have difficulty in emerging from hundreds of years when the Church was part of power and politics. The Church and the state were almost the same. Elsewhere Christians were abhorred, and their Christianity was denied. Some nonconformists opposed the institutions of the state on behalf of the oppressed, and we can look back to their traditions for the abolition of the slave trade, and campaigns about conditions in the mines, factories and sweat shops. Nonconformity was very influential in the formation of the Labour Party. Now many Christians are withdrawing from the close association between the Church and the state. They fail to see that by not taking a stand for the Gospel they are supporting the existing powers. These Christians say that they can have no contact with politics because it might corrupt them, and I would say that this is the majority view in the churches. The other two groups are those who still unequivocally side with the state, and those who equally strongly take this stand alongside the oppressed and poor. I belong to this third group, and I am bound to say that a reading of the Gospels leads me to this view. You cannot open Isaiah, Amos or indeed any part of the Bible, without coming to such a conclusion.

As well as being active at state or legislative levels, churches may get involved locally to improve conditions, perhaps working with local businesses. When businesses fail or leave, streets, houses and services deteriorate rapidly. Pastoring an unemployed community can be devastating, and in most urban areas jobs are like gold. Christians cannot afford to be neutral about them if they care about their families and their community. We can expect the retort, 'This is none of the Church's business!' Christians who believe in families, safety, employment, health, education, recreation and justice must minister to people and families, and work to improve their environment. Missionaries may have had many serious theological disagreements, but the most effective missions, whether 'liberal' or 'conservative', always had this in common: they demonstrated their offer of the Gospel with powerful deeds.

The Holy Spirit is doing his promised work among the poor, the prisoners, needy, outcasts, lonely, elderly and the unemployed, all over the world. The Spirit is showing up all around the neighbourhood, in churches and individuals. His effect can be seen in the growth of grass-roots community caring networks in some of the most run-down urban communities in the world. It is a wonderful sign of God's Kingdom in the city, that when the funding dried up and the professionals left, the Spirit sometimes moved in to continue the work he had begun before. Base communities of Christians are springing up in cities on all continents.

Clergy and laity: Nineteenth-century London gives us a wonderful laboratory to study the urban church on this issue of service. William Wilberforce (1759-1833) was an evangelically oriented layman who was counselled by John Newton to serve God in Parliament. He did so passionately and mobilised the anti-slavery movement. He was part of the Clapham Sect, a network of influential Anglican laity and clergy who developed urban and overseas activities. Many societies and programmes spun out of that group and much of the world was affected.

Lord Shaftesbury (1801-85) was another Christian lay public official whose career changed the way that London and other cities functioned, especially for the poor rural immigrants and industrialised millions who poured into them in the nineteenth century. Shaftesbury was a depressive throughout his life and sometimes could not work at all; yet he tenaciously pursued the agenda of social transformation that has benefited most of us in industrial cities to this day.

Charles Spurgeon (1834-92), a gifted Baptist preacher at Lóndon's Metropolitan Tabernacle, was a contemporary of Shaftesbury. These competent men served God within and outside traditional churches.

The New York experience parallels that of London. The Evangelical United Front was a coalition of public-spirited laity and visionary revivalists like Charles Grandison Finney. They promoted 'errands of mercy' with a passion and effectiveness hardly equalled in the history of the Church. In both London and New York the best church leaders worked with skilled laymen and women for evangelism and social change. It never occurred to those gifted believers that the clergy should do it all, or that evangelism and social action could be separated.

One of the principles of this book is that the work of the pastor is to equip and enable all Christians to be ministers. This applies especially to the duty of service at every level from relief to reform. I argue for a better trained clergy with biblical, historical, geographical and sociological competence, to complement lay people, not to replace them.

8
In the School and On the Street
Bringing up a family in the inner city

Relating urban and suburban churches

Having established that the laity have responsibility with the clergy for the plight of our urban churches, we can see that they cannot take up that responsibility if they are fleeing from the cities themselves.

For most Christians the cities are foreign and uncharted land which they view with great suspicion, fear and hostility. Christians have often written off the cities in the same way that the government has. The inner-city Christians must interpret the city to their suburban brothers and sisters. It is not just a matter of taking the city kids on trips to the countryside, but of bringing suburban Christians into the city to see for themselves, to discuss the issues of housing, policing and unemployment at first hand. Urban Christians must address themselves to the powerful suburban churches and persuade them that Jesus is not only our personal Saviour but also the Saviour of the world. Unless we are able to persuade sufficient numbers of people that things must change, there will be no change, and the divisions between poor and wealthy, black and white, employed and unemployed will increase.

The Church cannot change overnight from being the church of the powerful to that of the powerless without tensions and splits. We have people in our poor neighbourhoods following the Gospel with integrity, but the churches will not be healthy until we have some reconciliation and repentance, and until there is some coming together of urban and suburban churches. The Church is supposed to be a sign and an agent of the Kingdom; a divided Church is not a very effective sign. We must pray for reconcilers to tell suburban

Christians that they are not 'second-class Christians' because they live in the suburbs.

One example of reconciliation is the British system of 'twinning' churches from different types of community; many other options are possible. We must not, in any case, assume that every suburban Christian is skilled and fitted to work in the city. Many professional people could be retained as supporters and consultants to ministers and leaders, providing them with legal, financial, architectural, management and other skills. To those who are equipped for an urban ministry (whether ordained or lay) the call of Nehemiah can be made.

The question then is: 'How can Christians live as families and bring up their children in our most disturbed and dangerous neighbourhoods?'

The missionary family

I described earlier how Corean and I and our two sons Woody, four, and Brian, two, moved into a multiracial, gang-turfed section of Chicago in 1965. Many Christians have reproached us with endangering the education, morals or even lives of our children, and have regarded us as foolish.

They react differently to the story of Elisabeth Eliott. She is the wife of one of five martyrs who were drowned by tribesmen. She returned with her little daughter to live with the tribe who had killed her husband. She lived without walls, and with little other than a toothbrush. A picture in her book shows her little daughter on the shoulders of one of the men who killed her father, being taken across the river where he was drowned. When I shared that picture with evangelical Christians they responded with, 'Oh, what courage!'

It was a trauma for Corean and me to come from a rural area and let our young sons jump from house to house down the length of the street and play among the garbage cans. But my reading of missionary biographies showed me that our children could not be exempt from danger, and that missionary families often buried their children. Reading this history was very important for me and I became aware that we were one of a succession of families who gave up middle-class expectations for the sake of the Gospel. Our family would have to pay a price. Urban ministry is cross-cultural, and has more in common with the Two-thirds World than with the typical middle-class churches of America or Britain. We must draw our models from these more distant situations rather than from the middle-class church nearby. I have a cousin who lives in Africa with two children and they have puff-adders and cobras in the garden, and somehow that is heroic. We have cobras and pythons in Chicago too, but they are youth-gangs!

I demonstrated in Chapter 4 that the Bible reveals a God who loves cities and calls his people live in them, to carry out his redemptive work. If Christians insist that they can live and bring up their children only in suburbs, they are denying the Fall. So much evangelical piety survives only by living in gardens and extolling the superiority of suburbs or rural areas. This piety does not take seriously the biblical doctrine of sin.

If the churches are to flourish in our most disturbed urban areas, then Christians must learn to live and raise families in them. The churches need incomers, and we cannot just say that God will raise up new generations of Christians where there are none now. But incomers cannot with integrity call upon local Christians to stay put, if they themselves are planning to stay in inner London for five years before their escape to Surrey to bring up their children. The churches have traditionally been routes to material prosperity for their poor converts, who have been encouraged to use their new freedom in the Gospel to advance themselves, rather than to strengthen their fractured communities by remaining in them as salt and light.

Book-wise and street-wise

Life in the local school

For the benefit of my British readers I must explain that 'public schools' in America are run by local boards of education and funded by the government through local taxes. In poor neighbourhoods the public school is likely to be tough, multiracial, and to have a generally low level of academic achievement.

Private schools have had a long tradition in America because the various ethnic and religious groups wanted to teach their children in their own ways. During the nineteenth century this was countered by strong nationalistic feeling, and it was intended to educate all children to secondary-school level at public expense. However, from the 1950s onward the idea of national and equal education again became less popular. As the cities became more mixed racially, the white middle classes sent their children to private schools. Only 13% of families in Illinois send their children to public schools, and for most people, therefore, the public school system is of little interest. These schools are full of poor people and minorities and lack political influence.

Fundamentalist Christians are promoting independent Christian schools because of the 'secular humanism' of the public schools. We did not want our children to go to independent Christian, flag-waving schools, preferring them to experience diversity. There is not in fact 'secular humanism' in Chicago public schools, whatever else may be encountered. In our school there would be a black Pentecostal kid preaching in the lunch-hour and Ayatollah Khomeini supporters teaching Islam.

I could not afford to send the boys to private schools and even had I been able to do so, I would have been faced with an ethical issue. I could not send my kids to a paid school and pastor the kids of a congregation drawing social security. We decided to put our boys into the school with the other local children.

When the boys entered High School in 1974, armed policemen patrolled every hall and the washroom, which was unsafe to use. They also patrolled band contests and athletics meetings. My boys were athletes and played basketball and football. I had to fight my way into the school to watch them, and I was usually the only parent present. They had poor equipment, poor coaching, and swam in poor pools. I enjoyed lecturing at the school on history or civics, but I noticed that many of the books were published before the

Second World War. The school had had no new books for many years.

Whose responsibility? I regard my children as loaned to me as the gift of God. Parents have a primary responsibility for the way that their children are educated. Luther said that the first human institution which God created was the family. When the family broke down under pressure of sin, the law was introduced in Genesis 4. The law was to prevent Cain from devouring – or being devoured by – his family. It was to help the family, not replace it. There are three types of community – family (biological); state (geographical); and church (spiritual) – and I do not believe in the separation of these. The state does have a responsibility to educate the kids of my community – a responsibility it cannot pass to parents. Many children are refugees or come from single-parent or parentless homes. The state cannot allow these to miss their education because their parents are not around or aware.

Cities like Chicago were arguing in the 1970s that their schools were receiving victims of American foreign policy and were proliferating extra programmes for feeding, clothing and after-school care. The federal government should therefore take responsibility for these. Kennedy and Johnson agreed with these arguments, but the Reagan government is reducing public expenditure and cutting back the programmes. In the UK education cuts have produced enormous upheaval in schools. Teachers have gone on strike, not just for increases in pay, but in protest against the problems of working in an atmosphere of constant financial hardship, with buildings, equipment and books always in short supply.

I got involved with the school in many ways. I lunched with the boys and their friends in the cafeteria once a week. I watched their games, lectured classes, and did sports coaching. I was nominated to be a parent representative to evaluate the school as chairman of the Social Studies Sub-Committee. I interviewed seventeen teachers, some of whom had no books available, and many of whom were very committed, such as the teacher with multiple sclerosis, who taught from a wheelchair until the day before he died.

We helped our school to change the system of reports. Instead of sending the reports home with the children, the teachers invited parents to the school to meet them. They could then share with the parents how they could help their children in the various subjects, or tell them the bad news of their children's failure to tackle a subject. There have been good results and the system has now been extended to other schools.

Only by getting involved like this and networking power-coalitions throughout the city can Christians help to improve the education system. In our case we found that the Board of Education was not interested in the inner-city situation until a few white faces appeared at parents' meetings. Coalitions need to be built across class and racial lines to improve these schools. Because we sent our sons to an inner-city school and became extensively involved in it, we have been able to develop some influence.

Compensatory education

I studied the Jewish model for living in the city. In the ghettoes of Eastern Europe and America the Jews could not afford their own schools, and sent their children to common schools. However, they always added 'compensatory' education – the rabbi school, the Hebrew school in the weekend or evening, arts and music. I studied how Jews became first-class musicians, playing in the Chicago Symphony Orchestra while living in poor neighbourhoods. I began to see that it is not necessarily where you go to school that counts. People need a strategy for living in ghettoes, and the way the Jews set about it impressed me a great deal.

I sometimes pastored people who wished to remove their children from the public system and put them into private schools. I had a standard conversation, asking them what it would cost them. They would name a sum, the estimated cost for one, two or three children. I would then ask the people what sort of education system they could devise for their entire family for that sum each year. They could have a retreat every month, or a summer vacation to another country every year. They could buy all sorts of books and experiences. They could put a child in the Art Institute's ten-week summer school, or send him to a music camp. Why didn't they explore other options, keep their kids in the public school, and add some of these things?

Both Corean and I had survived bad schools, so we knew that it was possible. Her school had grades one to eight in the same room, and she really taught herself. Her mother wisely set her to reading novels, and she made her own world. Some children can cope with this; some teachers bring children into leadership at an early age by using the advanced ones as leaders.

Family life in the ghetto

I am arguing that we over-estimate the importance of schools against all the other institutions of the city, the city itself and the family in the education of our children. Chicago is full of museums and art galleries and we enrolled our children in the young artists' programme. On Saturdays they went by subway to paint and sculpt from a very early age.

We exposed them to the city. I took them to murder trials, courts, fires, disasters and riots, and got them involved with me in these things. When the children were six we decided they would have to master the city's public transport system. This would be equivalent to the rural skills of driving a tractor or milking a cow, which every boy of six or seven knows on an American farm. Our city is very large, and we would drop our children at different points in the city, give them a dime for a phone call, and tell them that if they arrived home by five o'clock without telephoning for instructions, they would get a free milk-shake. Well, I never got any phone calls, and I did have to buy a lot of milk-shakes. The kids at the age of six learned to get around the city on their own. Some parents panic when I tell them this.

Parental influence: During my consultations I have interviewed hundreds of pastors about the problems they have encountered in raising their families in difficult neighbourhoods. An English pastor said, 'How can I stop my own children becoming glue-sniffers and getting involved in vandalism and petty crime if they go out with the local estate kids? We have many children from broken homes whose parents do not look after them. I and my wife are clear that we want to identify with the community, but how far must our children be forced to identify with it?'

I have already suggested that both the provision of additional education resources – or 'cultural enrichment' – and close involvement of parents with the life of the schools will help the children to cope with the problems of the neighbourhood because they know that they are being supported. It has been widely established that children with strong bonds with their parents will derive their moral and behavioural values from their parents rather than from their peers. Corean and I built strong family ties and invested a lot of time in our children. I cut every church meeting except funerals to watch my sons' games. We decided that because we had boys I was the primary parent, and on Friday evenings I and my sons had a men's night out. We did not have much money but we would go for a swim, a milk-shake or a ride. I sometimes removed the children from school and took them with me on my activities such as ministers' meetings. Sunday evening was Corean's time with the boys. We ran family retreats and on each birthday we had parties in a hotel. These became traditions with the children and built up a close relationship between us. I could then ask them about the groups they were running with, and if I had to express my concern they would hear that loud and clear. We had a large reservoir of common experience to draw upon.

Meeting other children: I also decided that the best way to help my sons relate to the other children – without developing the bad behaviour feared by the English pastor – was to organise activities for the children of the same age as my own. I ran the Fairfield Kids' Club every summer for a month. Between 20 and 40 children each paid a dollar; they were given tee-shirts with different colours for each team. They were taken on trips, packed in a little van, and went to parks, another state, or a 747 aeroplane at O'Hare Airport. By running this programme, I became well respected in the community and my kids were looked up to. We were creating Christian culture among the group with whom our children related. When this group entered High School my children influenced them. I started the club as a strategy to protect my own children, but several members became Christians and formed the core of our church youth group.

By charging a little money and relieving parents for a little while, I also involved parents, and I got to know every child in the community by name. The children did things they would not otherwise have done, and the parents got a little breathing-space from the kids being round the house all day. Games, crafts, trips to the park, and athletics kept the kids too busy and involved to experiment with glue or drugs. We discussed these things and I showed them some films about drug-abuse. We also read Bible stories with them.

In 1968 Martin Luther King was murdered and there were widespread riots. I was angry because a great prophet had appeared and had been shot. My children were aged only five and seven but I took them with me into the riots, among the fires. I took softballs and bats and organised the black children into games. Night after night I took my boys into the riot area, found kids on the street and started playing ball. The old men came out to watch two small blond boys playing with all the black kids. We would play until it got dark. The bases would be a fire hydrant, a manhole cover, a parked car, a lamp-post, and so on. When we left in the car, they would ask us to return the next day. Our young children began to pray for these kids, and the fact of the black community burning down houses made a big impression on them.

Meeting individual needs: If Christians expect their churches and schools to meet all their needs – their own and their family's – they are being unrealistic and will probably make early departures from difficult ministries. They have to decide what each person's needs are and how these can be met. The city has many gifts for its people – music institutions, art and drama schools, evening classes and splendid events – more than enough to keep families alive and growing. The family in the city must ensure that each member has personal space to grow and develop, as well as her or his own networks.

Corean is an artist and musician and finds the city liberating. She would find life in an owner-occupied suburb stifling. However, in our early years in Chicago we lived next to the church and had a constant stream of visitors. This proved very difficult for Corean and we moved further away to give ourselves space. I had been too insensitive to my wife's needs, which could only be met outside the church.

Now we go to eight nights of opera during the autumn and to organ and choir music at several churches. Corean gives music programmes at home, perhaps a Russian, black, Spanish or German programme. At Christmas time we have a do-it-yourself singing of 'Messiah'. We invite our local store keepers, garage mechanics and others to these events. Classical music is not to many people's taste, but the pluralism of the city enables you to be yourself. Corean often practises for four hours daily on a 50-year-old grand piano which has been more than paid for by fees for lessons. She also did voluntary art work in the school for a day a week and was known by our kids' friends.

It is important to have a general philosophy of the urban pastor's family in its mission context. We must, however, adapt our principles to the needs of particular people, be they children or wives or husbands. The more messed up my community, and the more hectic my schedule, the more my home must be different from that – clean and quiet. I had an agreement with my wife that I would never come home angry about church politics and take it out on her. I get rid of my frustrations by riding my bike as hard as I can, going to a movie, to a local theatre, or just grabbing a newspaper and drinking coffee until I can come home and be civil. I always cool off first.

My own support systems were different from Corean's. For me to cope in the city I had to become multiracial and bilingual, and I discovered that I needed to study a different culture every year. In the first year I studied hillbillies, a culture from the Appalachian Mountains. In one of our vacations I went there and took a suitcase of books on Appalachian culture. We talked to local people in six of the poorest counties in the United States.

Our children did go through a period of resentment with our lifestyle when they were about 12 and 14. They resented having to live in a small, cramped apartment and sharing a common bedroom 10 feet by 12 with bunk-beds, when all their cousins had their own rooms. They also did not like us being broke for much of the time. When we replaced our first car with a four-door model, the boys claimed their own doors and divided ownership of the car as a street gang turfs an area.

Two Brians – black and white

When my elder son Woody was 14 he brought home a black friend from school – Brian. He was desperate, and the school thought that he would get into trouble. We did not set out to adopt him, and I tried to find him a suitable home. We did not have enough space or income and did not qualify for fostering aid. I went to parents I knew who had enough space and income, but nothing happened, so he moved in with us. Later I found his mother, who signed him away in court.

Black people in America have learned who they are and the theme that 'black is beautiful' has had a powerful effect. Brian never knew his father, and his mother rejected him; he has had to come to terms with that. Until he achieved a sense of identity, he would do bizarre things and dress in outlandish ways – looking good to cover up. His behaviour was a search for meaning.

We committed ourselves to bringing him up to connect with his scattered family. We spent a lot of time with various relatives who float in and out of Illinois. The anchor of his family is his great-grandmother who lives in Jackson, Mississippi, which is 800 miles from Chicago. We arranged for her to fly to Chicago – her first flight, at the age of 81. In the six hours we had together she told me and my wife many things. She was a Christian Big Mama in the classic black tradition and still teaches Sunday School in a black church. When I stay with her in Jackson I am the only white anywhere near that part of the town. She gave us a copper bucket and told us its story. 'This bucket was given to me by my grandmother, who was given it by her owner. I want you to have it until Brian is ready to receive it. Then I want you to tell him the story of our family.' I became the 'Keeper of the Bucket' and realised the importance of this symbol.

When Brian came to us, he had never had a father and had no idea what fathers did. When I left home for the first time for a teaching tour in Mexico, he was almost in panic, thinking that perhaps I was not coming back. This was the first time he had had a dad and he was losing him again. He kept asking Corean, 'Is dad coming home?'

To help Brian develop his capacity to make judgements we adopted a special system. When one of the boys did something wrong, the other two assigned the punishments. One night my younger Brian failed to turn up and there was panic on, because more than 30 boys had been murdered recently in our neighbourhood. We reported his absence to the police, and later he strolled in as though nothing had happened. My son Woody remembered that he had once been kept at home for three weeks for being one and a half hours late, so he wanted to give Brian the maximum sentence. Black Brian knew that he would often be in trouble and favoured keeping the sentence as low as possible. They therefore discussed his punishment in an interesting way, and finally ended up by making him stay at home for three weeks.

Encountering racism: I am a black father by adoption and have had to think through all these issues of race. It is not an easy matter, but we are in a neighbourhood which is more black than white. Our community is 28% black, 28% Asian, 21% Spanish. The minority in the High School the boys attended, and in the church, are white. There are many mixed-race marriages in our community, and in fact in our church it did not matter whom you dated. Mexicans dated blacks, blacks dated whites and so on. My three sons have all dated girls of different colours and racial backgrounds. In our community there is no problem with that.

Elsewhere, of course, things are different. One instance was in a Holiday Inn in Arkansas in the deep south – racist territory. We had been driving across Texas in temperatures of 90 degrees and more, when we saw a big swimming pool next to the Holiday Inn. The pool was full when I took my black son there; and for five minutes or so I was completely engrossed in teaching him how to swim. When I looked up, the pool was empty apart from Brian and me. All the white people had left the pool, and they were very angry to find me and my son in it. I realised for the first time that I was now implicated in racism, and subject to discrimination.

After Brian had been with us for about a year, he came to us after the other two had gone to bed and said that he wanted to become a Christian. His progress has been difficult, but he has come a long way, and was baptised into a black Baptist church in 1984.

When he came to us, Brian had never read a book, and he was several grades behind when he left High School. His grade did not qualify him for many colleges. I got him into a college on probation, and he lasted one year and dropped out for two. Now he is back in, has just finished his second year, and is doing very well. He is a youth minister, and in the summer works as a youth outreach minister in Washington DC.

Brian and I both hope that his story will encourage and help some of the readers of this book.

What our children learned

When we discovered that 87% of the world's people are yellow, black and brown, Corean and I wrestled with the question, 'Where can we raise our children where that reality exists?' We had two white sons at the time and the inner city of Chicago was ideal, because whites in our community were 13% of the total. We decided that it would be good for our boys to grow up aware of their own minority status as white people. If white children are not given this awareness, they may be educationally deficient, no matter how much science and mathematics they learn. The reality is that urban neighbourhoods may in fact be the best place to educate your children for life and service in the real global village.

Academic and social life: We often wondered whether we were right to send Woody and Brian to the local schools. Woody and black Brian graduated from High School with average marks which did not qualify them for the best colleges. Brian is an outstanding footballer and got many offers from what I call the 'flesh-markets' for footballers. I am practical, and when a strike meant that Brian would miss the football season in his senior year, I enrolled him in a Catholic school with an outstanding school team. The school was mostly black, and he was a minority white boy in the team. Coaches east of the Mississippi watched him play and made films of him, and this was why he got so many college offers. Now he is not interested in football but in theatre and art.

Despite their poor school and the inevitable childhood resentments, my children were far ahead of their peers in most respects. They got used to multiracial relationships and developed leadership skills. Reflecting on their upbringing now, they feel that they have had a super education. They know people from many different cultures, are culturally sensitive and came to know the Lord. When they got to college, they saw the parochialism of their student colleagues, who had never had black or oriental friends, and they didn't feel sorry at all. They arrived on the campus with much more global perspective than the other students.

Admittedly, it was their academic skills which suffered. In America this is not a real handicap because there are many colleges where you can enter at your own standard and progress at your own speed. All three boys are in college and in ministry. My youngest child did well at school, but he would have done so in any school. It was the other two who struggled with academic work.

Spiritual life: I cannot think of a time when Woody and Brian have not accepted the Gospel. Woody has always been a believer, has not wavered, and has led people to Christ. Brian has run a Young Life Club in Chicago during the summers. We prayed for them every night and read stories with them, including those of C S Lewis. They did not doubt the Gospel. They saw it lived, and that made the difference. They saw some gang kids transformed, and prayed for the black children they had played with during the riots. The people they respected most were the preachers who were holding the black community together. We would tell their stories, including that of Martin Luther King himself. These Christians were so impressive that my boys wanted to be like them. Now they are thinking of coming back to where we live. Woody would love to return as an inner-city teacher and coach. I am no longer a member of the church I pastored, and I and one of my sons go to a church in my local community. One of my sons stayed at the church I pastored. My wife and third son go to other churches. This is my story as a parent, a pastor and someone who works publicly with the education system.

I must end this section by warning against making children sacrificial lambs for abstract principles. In most cases the example of family enrichment I have described works, but there are some exceptions. The public schools of Chicago are not good with geniuses, and perhaps if your child is a genius you should put him into a special school. Gifted children are often temperamental, and may be younger than the others in their class. They may be ridiculed, beaten up or psychologically damaged. A second category are those with various handicaps. You must know your children and make wise decisions. One child might survive beautifully and keep his integrity, while another might be devastated.

Caring for families in the church

Barriers or bridges? Missionaries often report the benefits of having their children with them in their work. Children learn local languages and culture and make friends quickly. They reduce suspicion in communities normally closed to outsiders.

We saw ourselves as in the tradition of foreign missionaries, and our children were tremendous assets in the city. They learned the culture and became natives; they fitted immediately into the urban play networks. We were alien but our kids were in other people's homes and their kids were in ours. Because of them I was known as 'Woody's daddy' or 'Brian's daddy' and had immediate visibility in the community.

For many urban pastors, the family remains a barrier rather than a bridge to pastoral effectiveness. Some are afraid to expose their families to urban people, being willing only to give and not to take from them. We all know urban pastors who live in very pleasant areas, very far from the places they serve. I meet pastors who say, 'I would like to be an urban pastor, but I will wait until my kids leave school and then move in.' That's foolish in a way, because without the school networks and the children's networks you have a tremendous handicap in getting known.

The concept of family: The Christian nuclear family, living and flourishing in a disturbed urban neighbourhood, is a visible sign of the power of the Gospel we are offering. However, I do not agree with those evangelicals who have made the nuclear family the only concept of family. Ethnic families are extended families, and much of the city is characterised by multi-generational and multi-ethnic families. I don't hear the Church defending those.

Asians have had a multi-generational matrix for a long time. I was once with a group of Koreans in a class, when one man began to shed some tears about his family experience. His children were at school in the United States, and they had picked up a new idea, that the older you become, the more valueless you become. Too often the Church supports this with its idealisation of youth. This man had begun to see a kind of 'demonic' culture underlying American values. The Asians have for hundreds of years believed that the older you get, the more worthwhile you get, and the younger people serve the older. In the West, high mobility has created nuclear families where the older people are not only of little account, but may be scarcely known to the younger generations. The Western Christian family may have much to learn from cultures whose family structures are more stable than our own.

Responding to needs: The Church can do a great deal to bring both relief and reform in society on family issues. For example, a Yale study stated that the condition of an alcoholic may affect on average 34 members of a family. Thus if a church has a programme to help alcoholics, it is also helping all these members of each alcoholic's family. This is just one example of how through evangelism and pastoral care we can help many families and be a point of relief. When you help a teenager to keep out of prison, you help tax-payers as well as families! This is the normal ministry of the local church. It is not praised for it, nor is the work recognised. Our churches are doing this all the time – redeeming families, breaking the poverty cycle through God's gift of regeneration and discipleship. A church like this can produce a whole new quality of life in a community. The more you work with families, the more you realise you can use your collective leverage to change situations.

We must also deal with the mixed-race and single-parent families which abound in our inner cities. The city is anti-family, but the City which God is building is not, and this vision enables us to test the performance of our churches. We are trying to rebuild our communities through the Gospel. When a woman became a believer, I was very reluctant to instruct her to leave the person she lived with. He may well have been good to her or may have acted as a surrogate parent, and I could have caused harm by asking her to throw him out. Equally, married women were encouraged to stay with their husbands.

The biblical standard is monogamous, loving marriage – but in a first-generation mission situation it is not very loving to accept people, offer the grace of Jesus, and then clobber them with our views. Those who come to faith in an urban culture must be accepted as they are, just as we should accept, in a foreign culture, the tribal chief with five wives. We should not expect him to get rid of four of them. Which would he choose? What would happen to the others?

We responded to the needs of single-parent families in two ways. Firstly, I had a woman Associate Minister working with me in a pastoral team. We thought it most important to honour the principle that both male and female are created in the image of God, by having a shared man/woman ministry. Most people in the parish had never seen such a shared ministry before. Secondly, we prepared women to be executive heads of households. We ran training classes, job-development courses, and we took up a whole range of issues in the community. We realised that women are exploited at every level and often get only the lowest-paid jobs, without any insurance cover, injury benefit, or holiday pay.

Two stories from London

Elsie Lewis gives the following account of her work, meeting the needs of families in inner London.

> I have lived most of my life in Newham in inner East London. My family has been there for 200 years, digging and developing the docks, cutting the canals and building the houses. Newham has always suffered a lot, including extensive bombing in the last war. It is a run-down, working-class area.
>
> I moved away with my family from Newham for seven years. When we went, the youth group from the local church travelled out to the Sunday meetings at our house. It seemed incongruous to me and my husband that this should happen, and after hearing a poem by Michel Quoist in a service led by Colin Marchant, we decided to return to the borough. We knew that the cost would be high, but we believed that this was what the Lord wanted us to do.
>
> The children were then beginning school and I decided to get involved in the issues affecting local education. I encouraged the youth group to find out more about their own borough. They attended council meetings, and learned about the area in other ways. This helped to generate commitment: we now have 35 people serving the community throughout Newham, young people who have grown up through our youth group, who are staying put and doing things locally.

With other parents we mounted an extensive campaign, going on over many years, to draw the attention of the government and the Local Authority to the fact that Newham comes lowest of 103 boroughs by all kinds of educational criteria. As a result of the campaign, 100 schools now have Parent-Teacher Associations, and there are parent representatives on the Education Committee, and parent governors on each School Board. Five schools have been rebuilt, and we exerted pressure on the Department of Education and Science which was partially responsible, in conjunction with pressure from the trade unions, for the establishment of the Social Priority Allowance which gives additional financial resources to schools in the inner cities.

We have paid a cost. Our children are not being stretched as they might have been at a school with a better record of achievement, and one son has been beaten up. However, they have learned survival and other skills that they would not have learned in the suburbs. They have also been successful academically: one son has a degree, another a diploma in violin making, and two others are still at school. Although there are no jobs in East London, they are determined to stay in the local community, and so they are serving on a voluntary programme at a Christian Outdoor Pursuits Centre.

Research carried out through the United Nations shows that where you as a parent support your children and get on well with them, they will take their values from you. I do not think that Christian parents should be afraid of coming to the inner city with their children and bringing them up there. Our children have gained an enormous amount from growing up in Newham, and I say to people coming in, 'If you want to make significant changes, you have to stay for a long time.' Community groups which have been in existence for ten years or more are the ones which are achieving significant change.

Schools do sometimes have to provide facilities which

a home should normally offer. I have known children who have never handled a book, had a holiday or even been outside the borough before they come to school. They tend not to achieve high standards because they lack stimulus and are not supported at home. Under these conditions it is up to the schools – and the churches – to provide security and opportunities. When children themselves become parents they may sit down with their own children and read with them and share what they have learned, so a longer perspective is important. I saw a lovely lady on the bus the other day doing just that – reading with her little girl as she came home from school. Parents are the first educators. We have to enable them to fulfil that role.

One important development has been the establishing of a shop, with a current annual turnover of £250,000, which provides good play and teaching materials together with advice and support for parents, teachers and others in the work of education. Called the Parents Education Centre, it also offers a tea and chat room, and a drop-in centre for mothers with handicapped children; people come not only because they have a problem, but because it is a place where they may choose a book and enter a warm, friendly, welcoming environment. A second Centre has now been established in the Docklands area, working with the handicapped, providing literacy support on a one-to-one basis, helping with care for the under-fives and setting up women's educational programmes. From this Centre specially trained workers go out into the community, seeking to meet the acute local needs. They go to all kinds of unlikely places like the Port of London Authority, with play equipment, talking to mothers and showing them how to use the materials. This is part of a long process of helping mothers to enlarge their own vocabularies and horizons, and hence those of their children.

When we first moved into the area, we took responsibility for a lot of things, but now I don't have to run the play schemes, because there are younger local people willing to do so. The parents' groups, too, are able to organise themselves. People who have been in action campaigns are never the same again. They had never realised that they could run meetings and carry through campaigns, but now they have become politically aware and have learned how to bring about change. They are taking decisions about their own lives, and seeing themselves as valuable – just as Christ does.

Elsie Lewis' inspiring story shows all the benefits which Christian families can bring to inner-city neighbourhoods and also to themselves. Her family worked at a variety of levels from individuals to government, and saw people added to the family of God. I will end this chapter with the testimony of another London mother, Muriel Purkiss:

> Peter and I moved in 1973 with our three daughters aged 11 to 14, from the Kent side of Greenwich into inner London. I don't know that people felt that Peter was being very responsible, in moving in such a way, when our daughters were of that particular age, but we did move and we have been immensely grateful that we didn't make excuses to God about all the reasons why it was not wise and sensible to do what we did. Our daughters are very different now; they have learned such a lot, and have come to a really robust Christian faith which is not by any means a carbon-copy of ours. Had we not been obedient to what God called us to do, we might have been in a very different situation!

I hope that other Christian families will hear the call of Nehemiah and move into the desperate and disturbed cities of the world.

9
Networking the World
International urban ministry

An expanding ministry

Our church had started a Spanish Sunday School before I came. During my time there it became so big that the building could not accommodate any more. We started a Spanish-speaking daughter church, and seven other churches sprang out of Fairfield in my first five years. Corean had studied some German but we now found ourselves requiring Spanish, which I learned from a neighbouring pastor. We founded a Spanish seminary, which now has 100 students.

However, in spite of this pressure to become multilingual, I still had no idea that eventually I would be doing international work, and organising Third-world studies in inner Chicago. My next move was to work on a board for Palestinian rights – an unpopular cause in the United States, and one which arouses a great deal of hostility.

In 1975 I joined the Northern Baptist Theological Seminary, because I shared the vision of the President who was a friend of mine. He wanted the seminary to be intercultural, interracial and international. I teach missiology, urban evangelism and church history. We are trying to build a caring community on the campus which will help our future pastors to care effectively for urban and rural neighbourhoods.

Seminary Consortium for Urban Pastoral Education

A few years ago I started to talk with other people about training urban pastors, because we had seen so many burn out. We put together a programme called SCUPE – Seminary Consortium for Urban Pastoral Education. This is a network of 10 seminaries which place their students in the city during the second or third years of the Master of Divinity course. We also use it with the Northern Baptist Doctor of Ministry programmes. In 1985 a review of SCUPE graduates showed that most were working in cross-cultural situations, many of them with or under blacks or Hispanics. Two-thirds of them work in parishes, and the rest in social agencies like local community action groups or Jesse Jackson's Operation Push. Classes take place on two days a week, when we teach courses like cross-cultural communications, urban church history, urban culture, urban evangelism, systems, finance, and how to use credit and banks to help urban communities. In our course on urban transition students interview pastors who have seen their area go through racial or cultural change, and try to assess the patterns. What activities went well and what didn't? Why did this one succeed, and not that? We do not call this urban training. To me, education is about presenting students with many options, and it assumes their discretion.

We aim in SCUPE to teach these skills:

1. How to acquire a working knowledge of the systems, issues and population trends of a large city.
2. How to communicate with people from different racial and ethnic backgrounds.
3. How to analyse an urban neighbourhood and identify its needs, concerns and resources.
4. How to identify the existing lines of authority in an urban church.
5. How to interpret scripture to show the implications for the urban environment.
6. How to develop working relationships with the social agencies in the community.
7. How to write applications for funds.
8. How to decide whether to play a supporting or leadership role in each situation.
9. How to apply one's training in sociology, theology and ministry to major social issues.
10. How to work constructively with a church in decline.
11. How to lead a church in effective outreach which will help an urban community.
12. How to work with the political, economic and social structures of an urban society so that they are influenced by the values of God's Kingdom.

SCUPE seeks to add these skills to existing college and ministry experience. One of our seminars is preceded by the students visiting a different ethnic neighbourhood for six hours, including eating a meal in a local restaurant. During the seminar we discuss the experience and the community's characteristics. In this school without walls, students visit banks, city hall, prisons, neighbourhood organisations and a host of ministries, in order to engage leaders in critical reflection on ministry in those diverse contexts.

One of the most significant visits is to our inner-city High School where there are 2,300 teenagers, over half of whom are foreign born, from 50 nations of the world. At one time the school prepared mostly Jewish and Scandinavian children for college, but now it is an entry school for migrants and refugees who study in nearly a dozen different languages and learn English only partially. The head teacher and his staff survive because they have developed a global meanings-system; they are strong, secure people; they have decentralised their programmes; and they have learned to live with great difficulties. The school is an educational marvel, and a model of what the urban church ought to be in that community. God is using a school to witness to the Church about its own nature and mission in the city.

The international perspective

The Lausanne Covenant

In 1974 around 3,000 delegates and 1,000 observers, representing the Church on all continents and all denominations, gathered at Lausanne, Switzerland. They met to articulate afresh the task of world evangelisation in our generation. The Covenant they agreed says to the churches, in effect, 'For too long you have waited for the Church in the West to do the work in traditional Western ways. You've decided that white people should lead the Church in mission, and have failed to see that the Two-thirds World churches have mission responsibilities too.'

In the past century of international urban ministry, the Church in the West has generally provided the capital and the programme for the cities of the world. Giants like John R Mott went to cities to plant the YMCA or other ministries. The move was from West to East. It presupposed that the theology and strategy of the Western cities was universally appropriate, and that the Western denominations should expand, building their urban headquarters from which ministry would flow out of the city into the countryside. However, this scheme is out of place in the modern world. It is time for a new day in the world mission of the urban church: indigenous groups, with leaders accountable to them and to their church in the city, should claim the whole city in the strong name of Jesus Christ. It is time for urban church people to reach out in love to the new believers who have the same Spirit, but different cultures and forms. It is time for people to gather and pray specifically for the cities of the world and God's mission within them. God help us to do it.

The first consultations: In 1980 the Lausanne Committee for World Evangelisation convened a consultation at Pattaya, Thailand. This mini-consultation on the evangelisation of large cities had 110 delegates, and was chaired by me. I was appointed as Associate to co-ordinate and service an extensive programme of consultations on urban ministry around the world. Between 1980 and 1985 I participated in a variety of consultations in 80 large cities on all continents. I have listened to pastors in the rapidly developing cities of the Two-thirds World and to those of the old developed countries, and most have admitted that they have not been equipped for urban ministry.

In my consultations I try to bring together the diversity and unity of the Church: the variety of church forms and structures on the one hand, and on the other, the unity of God's people in their biblical calling, which is the same everywhere and at all times. Christians in the largest cities of the world should see themselves as a global ministry team. This is no appeal for ecclesiastical unification, but is much more realistic, practical and significant. We can come together first in our own cities and explore ways to share our concerns and resources; raise questions about our urban mission, and suggest some ways of addressing them.

My hope is that every urban Christian will experience and promote both the local mission of the global church and the global mission of the local church. They are the two sides of our urban missionary coin. If our God continues both to urbanise his world and to internationalise his cities, we shall meet each other most concretely in the urban ministry of the Church. Perhaps no greater vision or more profound hope can keep us faithful in our pastoral tasks. Let us celebrate Kingdom unity in our respective cities. Our Lord is asking the urban church to be and do much in this turbulent world, and inevitably we shall touch each other in his service.

Calling Christians together

The scene is Copenhagen, 1985. It might be in several score of other cities anywhere in the world. Around 40 key leaders from different ministries and denominations have met to talk in a climate of openness and sharing. They represent four key groups: pastors, mission-agency people (social workers, youth workers, or members of organisations like Youth for Christ), lay people with a vision, and staff of theological colleges or leadership trainers. I have found everywhere that these groups feel isolated from each other. They do not meet or talk together, and often experience their brothers and sisters in Christ as threats rather than supports. The Copenhagen consultation begins by calling together a group of people who understand that the Kingdom of God is bigger than their ministries, churches or traditions. The Kingdom is God's vision and action in the world, and we need Kingdom people to build bridges and tear down barriers between us, so that the whole city can hear the Gospel.

Meeting each other: The Christians begin by talking to each other in groups of four or five with these questions:

Who are you?
Why have you come?
What is the most exciting thing in your ministry now?

What is the most discouraging thing you are facing?

What specific things do you hope to get from this consultation?

The group develops its agenda for a three-day event from the last question.

An important component of the consultation is the carefully constructed day-long tour of the city, with introductions to its history, districts, food and ministries. On the second day the group goes out like this to explore other ministries, a thing pastors resist for many reasons. I send mainline ministers to evangelical churches, and vice versa. People create energy and break down barriers because they realise that they did not know their city nor what God was doing in it. The groups may visit four ministries in a day and return euphoric, irrepressible. They are like the disciples returning to Jesus after he had sent them to the cities.

The urban church leaders have discovered, often for the first time, what is happening in their city – all the different ways God's people are evangelising in Jesus' name. Much of the euphoria comes from the fact that they learned it by themselves and from each other across denominational, colour, class and linguistic barriers. This celebration of what God is doing in their city gives the group 'permission', new motivation, and energy to invent strategies for additional creative ministries and resources. It is interesting to see people pair up to check diaries and follow up common interests. Healing and empowering can begin in this way, if one trusted bridge-builder calls the leaders into a network; God confirms this call over and over. Perhaps you can do this in your city.

Gaining a vision: On the third day the group begins to plan. Who is not being reached in this city? Who are the really poor and needy? What are the barriers which keep us from evangelising our city? My rôle is not to come with a glossy, prepackaged solution, but to be a facilitator and resource person for the committees which have been convened. I try to deal with barriers to evangelism by telling the groups about SCUPE, giving a liberating word, and suggesting urban curricula, resources and books. I want these committees to be as broad as possible, from fundamentalist to radical, and everybody in between.

In spite of the unique cosmic issues facing today's Church, most major pastoral issues have surfaced before. One of the tasks of these consultations (as of any urban ministry training) is to identify with this history and learn from it. Otherwise we are doomed to make all the mistakes again, and too many urban Christians have done so.

Most Christians accept a biblical standard, but often will not admit it because the Bible was taught in their city in such a narrow, negative and simplistic way. They do not want to be caught using the same language or even the same Bible. In the consultations I am trying to create a climate in which people see that the biblical vision is much broader than they may have thought.

I have found it best not to start from the ideal – 'What should our ministry look like?' but from guided explorations into 'What does our ministry look like in this city?' We then work back in analysis to the ideal. It is better to take people to the Parthenon than to lecture on Greek temples. They can then say, 'What a magnificent ruin!' and imagine what it once looked like. If I were to lecture on the ideal nature and types of urban ministry, this would be experienced by participants as a paternalistic put-down, inducing guilt. Instead, the consultation process encourages urban workers to observe or 'read' models of ministry and then reflect upon them. Lifelong change and growth can then occur.

Partners in mission: The urban church has been fractured by divisions of doctrine, language, race, class and many other dynamics, rooted in history and in people's insecurity and rivalry. The consultation helps to recall Christians to the vision of the redeemed city and to empower 'the whole Church to take the whole Gospel to the whole city'. The purpose of the consultation is to help people towards a series of aims:

1. Fellowship. People hurt for a variety of reasons and

the consultations are designed to be pastoral and caring.

2. Learning. We learn from each other what God is teaching us. This city is our laboratory of models which we can study and reflect upon.
3. Gaining a vision. This is the essential ingredient for reaching the city.
4. Sharing resources. These are biblical, historical, geographical and congregational. Some of the experiences of fellow believers include a host of evangelisation models, strategies and skills which can be shared.
5. Strategic planning. Good planning for future mission may then take place on a shared basis.

My world-wide consultations have reinforced the basic principles of urban mission: that great cities are international, and their social and cross-cultural difficulties are the same everywhere. In cities scattered across the globe I have been told about the same mission issues:

1. Charismatic renewal is a fact of urban life, and God's Spirit is blowing in some surprising places. This renewal brings life and hope to many; questions, problems, jealousy and apparently schism to others. Many sense that God is doing something remarkable that the Church hierarchies have not been able to accept.
2. Narrow denominationalism is hampering: many evangelicals admitted that they learned some of their most significant lessons for urban ministry from Roman Catholics on the one hand and sectarians on the other.
3. Many urban churches or para-church ministries have been shown to be culturally captive. They are so dependent upon a unique economic or cultural context or key leader, that inevitable changes in the context have doomed the ministries because they could not or would not adapt. Many successful

models have sociological as well as theological explanations.

4. Cities serve to make visible the most difficult human needs, and study groups all over the world are calling for church-wide sensitivity to the poor, especially those in structured poverty, i.e. poverty caused by rapid industrialisation, dislocation, famine, policies of greed and revolution. We hear calls for both relief strategies and reform as partners in the task of urban evangelisation.
5. Some groups call for new structures to bridge urban and non-urban resources so that large-city mission may be less hampered by lack of resources, both financial and human.
6. Many groups affirm the need for para-church ministries in consciousness-raising and co-ordinating roles. Such ministries model the presence of the Kingdom.
7. Fellowships must achieve greater depths of emotion, commitment and personal caring at all levels of human relationships in cities. This is needed more, perhaps, than in other places, to compensate for the environmental turbulence and trauma the city introduces to family systems, personal health and Christian growth. Discipleship and community must be the goal of evangelisation.

Ministers from widely separated countries have reiterated these same problems and arrived at the same conclusions. Because of this, the old West-to-East model of mission is outdated: nowadays, we are all partners in mission, sharing our insights and benefiting from each other's experience.

10
Do It Yourself
Equipping your church for its task

This chapter contains six exercises I have developed, together with a Training Issues Checklist by Jim Hart, to help you put the ideas of this book into practice. Some apply mainly to pastors; others to church leaders of all kinds; others to groups and committees; others to families. Whatever you do in the Family of God, you need personal support and motivation. Issues like 'authoritarian leadership', 'support' and 'burn-out' often occur in the checklist, as they apply to pastors, but they are important for all Christians. Pressure to reform churches and ministries may come as much from church members as from committees and pastors. Equally, reforms suggested by pastors or committees will fail unless the vision for them is communicated to, and shared by the whole Body.

Six exercises

Pictures of the Church

There are many images of the Church in the Bible and in people's minds. This study is designed to stretch vision, and may provide permission to launch mission on a broad front. It will also help any church to understand why its members are so often in conflict. Each image carries different expectations of the pastor, and of the mission of the church.

The exercise is a delightful and helpful way of introducing profound insights. It is good to preach from the Bible about the ideal church, but people will learn more quickly by studying these concrete images for themselves. A non-threatening climate for dealing with conflicts is created.

Write the following list on your board:

Pictures of the church

Army	Community	Migrant group
Body	Embassy	Mission
Building	Expeditionary	People
Business	force	Priesthood
Castle	Family	Retreat centre
Clinic	Halfway house	Sacrament
Colony	Herald	School
Communications	Lifeboat	Servant
centre	Lighthouse	Team

Ask the group to select one of the words and ask them these questions in turn:

What sort of environment does it suggest?
What view of the Gospel does it suggest?
What is the role of the church member?
What is the role of the minister?

They might pick the word 'clinic'. They regard the environment, and perhaps the church members, as sick. The Gospel is the healing medicine. Are church members the patients or the healers? Is the minister the only healer? They can study the other words from the list which appeal to them.

Evaluating models of ministry

People who talk about urban ministry frequently get asked questions such as:

Which church is right?
Could you give me some of the best examples of urban ministry?
What is your programme?
How large should an urban church be?
Which urban church models grow best?
Is not [a specifically named church] how we ought to do urban ministry?

Many people want answers to what seems to be an urban ecclesiastical riddle, but when you probe the questioners, the assumption usually emerges that there must be one key strategy that will provide the single solution to 'reaching the city', and that the existing ways of ministering are either wrong or ineffective.

This exercise explores contemporary models of ministry in your city or neighbourhood. Teams can be sent out from a consultation which you have convened, or groups from two churches could agree to exchange visits. Teams are sent to denominationally diverse churches and para-church programmes, which may include such exposures as a traditional church, a drug programme, housing estate evangelism, new church development strategy or a base community ministry. If team members come from different denominations themselves, they seldom view models in the same way because their own theological and psychological lenses select and filter observations differently.

The set of questions could well be studied by your own congregation or by one of its groups or committees. Do not visit another church to be critical. Its ministry will be very different from yours, and that is part of what you will learn. It will be reaching people that you do not. You will learn that there is variety and diversity in the Body of Christ, and will share new ways of tackling common problems together.

The visitors ask the host church the following questions:

1. What is the unique context of this ministry? Walk around the community to observe. Ask questions. Could you point out the special features of this area?
2. What is the history of this ministry? What was the founder's vision? What have been the failures and successes? What steps led to the present programme?
3. What is the programme? Where is it held, and on what days/times? Does it use one setting or scattered locations?

4. How is it organised? Who is accountable to whom? Where are decisions made and by whom?

5. What does it cost? Who pays for it? Is the money found locally, from members, from clients, from denominations or from other grant sources?

6. What is the theological basis for this ministry? Probe beneath such likely responses as 'the Great Commission' to identify the theological themes and goals important to this model. The Great Commission gets blamed for a great deal of stupid urban ministry, and many people do not know how to think theologically about their work.

7. Whom are you trying to reach? Analyse the class, race, age and sex profiles of the ministry and compare them with the community profile of the first question. How are they similar, and how different? Are you trying to reach prostitutes, juvenile delinquents, first offenders, divorced people, night people, the unemployed, the elderly, children, Moroccans, students, businessmen, politicians? Is there one group, several groups, a sub-group or a major group?

8. What skills do the leaders have? What would I need to learn in order to do what you do? What skills could I learn by watching you? You may have worked with drug addicts and know a lot more about drugs than I do. How are the leaders' skills being taught in this programme? How is leadership developed in this model?

9. What does this ministry do well, and what does it leave undone? The observer must try to distinguish between the value of the model and the way it is used here. What are the strengths and the weaknesses of the model itself? An example would be a programme which uses rock music to share the Gospel with teenagers. This will probably alienate old people. The very strength of the ministry to one

group is also a weakness which limits it from reaching other groups.

10. What is the future of the ministry? What scenarios can you imagine? How could it be adapted to meet the contextual changes we can predict?

Urban mission strategies

The mere existence of models and strategies does not guarantee health and vitality. Some cities have them in place, but they are not functioning with vision, compassion, competence, and in the strong name of Jesus Christ. Programmes are no substitute for the Holy Spirit, but the Spirit's presence will be evidenced in both persons and programmes.

Which programme, model or strategy is right? What is your programme? God has given us urban ministry resources and pastoral tool kits as large and diverse as the city itself.

The following list of sixteen strategies for urban mission will give you ideas or point you to para-church or denominational agencies which could help your church with that particular strategy.

1. Arts strategies. Ministries by urban artists use visual, musical and dramatic arts to communicate the Gospel.
2. Age group strategies. Ministries and some specialised organisations isolate one age group and direct their programme expertise to children, youth, the elderly, single people, professional people, etc.
3. Economic development strategies. Many urban ministry groups go beyond initial relief and disaster programmes to develop projects that teach employment skills, or provide housing, health, education, food or financial skills, and take up environmental issues.
4. Ecumenical strategies. Many urban ministry groups share evangelism programmes, leadership develop-

ment events and combined worship at special seasons. Access to public institutions or political campaigning usually require ecumenical co-operation.

5. Educational strategies. New models of lay training and college education are emerging in many cities.

6. Mass evangelism strategies. Mass movements have great power, whether it be a papal mass with a million present in a stadium, or a rally led by Billy Graham. Urban powerlessness and alienation have often formed the background for massive meetings, especially where the Christian community in a city is small.

7. Institutional strategies. Some ministries witness to and within hospitals, gaols, universities, secondary and professional schools, homes for the aged or other institutionalised groups.

8. Language strategies. It is often possible to reach across culture and language barriers with literature or other media.

9. Lay strategies. Special ministries seek to identify, equip and empower lay ministries within their vocations, and collectively in the city.

10. Media strategies. Some ministries are committed to public communication processes in electronic and print media.

11. New church development strategies. Many local churches intentionally plan to multiply new ones, but other churches start by deliberate, para-church development.

12. Political strategies. The city is a political system, and frequently a corrupt one. Churches often try to affect political issues, and sometimes go beyond that to create alternative political structures that are more just.

13. Recreational strategies. Some ministries use athletics and athletes in the city.
14. Relief strategies. These range from local church food kitchens, clothing banks and shelter care to massive international caring programmes.
15. Revitalisation strategies. Church groups often serve as the catalyst for the creation and renewal of neighbourhood organisations. At another level, there are para-church ministries that exist for the renewal of the church and function prophetically and pastorally to Christians and churches.
16. Solidarity strategies. This is a ministry as old as Paul, who took offerings from daughter churches to support the mother church in Jerusalem. The Church is now globally significant and the churches of the city can and do express solidarity on a broad range of concerns with believers in other parts of the world, or of different social backgrounds.

Mapping the congregation

Urban churches, especially small ones, tend to move towards informal – or tribal – methods of making decisions, whatever the church constitution may prescribe. Pastors do best not to try to enforce constitutions rigidly, but to map their congregations and seek to find out accurately what is happening. Urban congregational life is complicated and things change slowly, so that to define the existing situation accurately may be more important than action and decisions. The pastor as manager may be unable to do much about some things and needs to learn to live with ambiguity. The mapping exercise is designed for pastors and the simple steps are set out below.

Make a 'who does what' chart:

1. Identify officers, including yourself, and each group, formal or informal, including Sunday School groups.

2. List their functions as formally defined in the constitution.
3. Discuss their functions with them and decide together what they actually do.
4. See if there are differences between who should be performing some specific function and who actually is doing it. Seek to understand the dynamics.

Make a map of the congregation:

1. Draw a diagram of the congregation where you are. Put the major (or power) group near the centre.
2. Label the parts most affected by history and tradition with blue. This might be a class in the Sunday School, a board or committee.
3. Label the parts most affected by the immediate environment with red.
4. Map the formal or informal communications systems with solid green lines, and the informal communications systems with dotted green lines.
5. Map the formal decision-making systems with red lines and the informal ones with black lines.
6. Label with dotted green circles the parts which are most likely to work with you to achieve your goals.
7. Label with dotted red circles the parts which are most likely to be troublesome to you.
8. Identify with red asterisks any persons who are troublesome to you in any parts of the organisation.

Design an intervention strategy: Analyse what you have learned about the church's behaviour from the map. Areas of concern might include:

Leadership patterns
Worship

Relationship of various parts to the whole
Decision-making
Communication
Goals (quality and direction)
Structural arrangements
Relation to community
Mission involvements
Climate or internal character of the church.

From the two earlier exercises, identify the group or individuals with whom you would begin a revitalisation process, and outline what you think this process might involve.

Questions for urban ministry colleagues

1. Can we study together the historic and contemporary ministry of the whole church in our city?
2. How can we generate security, identity, commitment and energy in a group which crosses denominational, racial and linguistic boundaries?
3. Can we put together a working directory of ministry strategies, models and resources for our city?
4. Which sectors of the city, and which groups of people are being touched in some significant ways by ministry, and how is it being done?
5. Can we prepare case studies of ministries to share together?
6. Which groups have no significant contact with the churches' ministries? Who can be called the 'unreached'?
7. What would the church look like if those groups were to be reached by the Gospel and followed up by effective ministry?
8. What resources do we need for new ministries and the renewal of existing ones?

9. What ministry knowledge and skills have we already got between us and how can we share these together?

Praying for your city and your world

A group of pastors in Washington DC have a globe, and every week they pray for a different city of the world. A group in Amsterdam goes on prayer walks around the city. Walk around your neighbourhood looking at people and praying for them. Different church members can be assigned to streets in the community and encouraged to walk along them and pray for everybody there. In Columbia, South Carolina, we climbed a hill outside the city and prayed for every section and for those who were ministering there. This was a very significant time of worship, committing the city to God and praying that we would be given the compassion needed to reach it.

Training issues checklist

This is a checklist to enable the reader to pick out quickly areas for personal consideration. It does not require particular kinds of answer, merely an awareness that a topic is relevant to your situation, and that a rereading of the chapter concerned could be used to guide your own thinking and decision-making, or those of a group, committee or the whole church. (There are no questions for Chapter 2.)

Chapter 1
Do I have a vision for urban ministry?
Have I attempted to study my immediate environment?

Chapter 3
Is there a mission field in my neighbourhood?
Is our church evangelising or merely poaching members from other denominations?
Is my attitude to problems prescriptive or diagnostic?
Is our church adopting an authoritarian style of leadership?
Do I try to improve social conditions in my area?
Have we changed our church traditions to break down the barriers for outsiders?

Are we over-involved in impersonal programmes?
Have we analysed the barriers to mission in our locality?

Chapter 4
Have I accepted my city as a sacred place where God is working?
Do I pray regularly for my own and other cities?
Have I studied the biblical lessons for pastoral leaders?
Has our church welcomed those of other races and faiths with hospitality?
Have we combined evangelism with social action?

Chapter 5
Is there a core group of faithful members in our congregation?
Is there a danger that they may feel threatened by newcomers?
Can we create a vision for the future in our church?
Are there useful skills we could teach our church members?
Do we share decision-making?
Do we encourage members to minister to their own networks of relationships?
Do we accept people whose lives do not conform to our standards of Christian behaviour?

Chapter 6
Do I know my neighbourhood, and the needs of the various groups within it?
Do we have good relationships with other churches in the area?
Do we have good relationships with the social agencies in the area?
Does the pastor have a clear system of priorities to help avoid overload?
Does the pastor share the work with a suitable staff team?
Does the pastor have a personal support group?

Chapter 7
Do our members know what kind of church they are looking for?
Do we know what kind of church we want to be?
Do we relate sympathetically to the cultures around us?

Do we recognise and deal with racism in ourselves?
Do we relate sympathetically to Christians of other cultures?
Does our worship fulfil its biblical purpose?
Is our worship designed for our congregation?
Does our preaching relate scripture to the life of the church members?
Do we train individuals for personal evangelism?
Do we model our fellowship on Acts 2?
Do we work for relief and reform in our community?

Chapter 8
Are we willing to live and work in the city?
Do we trust God to safeguard and nurture our children?
Have we considered how we can supplement formal education?
Do we consider and try to meet the needs of each member of the family?
Do we see family life as a barrier or a bridge to pastoral effectiveness?

Chapter 9
Could ministry in our city be improved by consultations?

Bibliography

Abell, Aaron Ignatius. THE URBAN IMPACT ON AMERICAN PROTESTANTISM 1865-1900. London: Archon, 1962.

Agnew, John. Mercer, John and Sopher, David, eds. THE CITY IN CULTURAL CONTEXT. Boston: Allen & Unwin, 1984.

Barrett, David B. WORLD CHRISTIAN ENCYCLOPEDIA. Oxford: Oxford University Press, 1982.

Berry, Brian J. L. ed. URBANIZATION AND COUNTER-URBANIZATION. Urban Affairs Annual Reviews, Vol. 11, Beverly Hills, CA: Sage Publications, 1976.

Butterworth, Douglas and Chance, John K. LATIN AMERICAN URBANIZATION. Cambridge: Cambridge University Press, 1981.

Callow, Alexander B. Jr., ed. AMERICAN URBAN HISTORY. Oxford: Oxford University Press, 1982.

Claerbaut, David. URBAN MINISTRY. Grand Rapids, MI: Zondervan, 1983.

Dayton, Edward R. and Wilson, Dr. Samuel. eds. UNREACHED PEOPLES 82. Elgin, IL: David C. Cook, 1982.

Dougherty, James. THE FIVESQUARE CITY. Notre Dame, IN: Notre Dame Press, 1980.

Fava, Sylvia Fleis. URBANISM IN WORLD PERSPECTIVE: A READER. New York: Thomas Y. Crowell Co., 1968.

Gugler, Josef and Flanagan, William D. URBANIZATION AND SOCIAL CHANGE IN WEST AFRICA. Cambridge: Cambridge University Press, 1978.

Hall, Peter, ed. THE INNER CITY IN CONTEXT. London: Heinemann, 1981.

Herington. John. THE OUTER CITY. London: Harper & Row, 1984.

Jacobs, Jane. CITIES AND THE WEALTH OF NATIONS. New York: Random House, 1984, and Viking: London, 1985.

Kelley, Allen and Williamson, Jeffrey G. WHAT DRIVES THIRD WORLD CITIES' GROWTH? Princeton, NJ: Princeton University Press, 1984.
Krupat, Edward. PEOPLE IN CITIES. Cambridge: Cambridge University Press, 1985.
Marchant, Colin. SIGNS IN THE CITY. London: Hodder & Stoughton, 1985.
Miller, Randall M. and Marzik, Thomas D., eds. IMMIGRANTS AND RELIGION IN URBAN AMERICA. Philadelphia: Temple University Press, 1977.
Newland, Kathleen. CITY LIMITS: EMERGING CONSTRAINTS ON URBAN GROWTH. Worldwatch Paper 38, 1980.
Norwood, Frederick A. STRANGERS AND EXILES. Vols I and II. Nashville: Abingdon, 1969.
Palen, J. John. THE URBAN WORLD. New York: McGraw Hill, 1981.
Pasquariello, Ronald; Shriver, Donald W. Jr. and Geyer, Alan. REDEEMING THE CITY. New York: Pilgrim Press, 1982.
Perlman, Janice E. THE MYTH OF MARGINALITY. Berkeley, CA: University of California Press, 1976.
Portes, Alejandro and Walton, John. URBAN LATIN AMERICA. Austin, TX: University of Texas Press, 1976.
Sjoberg, Gideon. THE PREINDUSTRIAL CITY. London: Collier Macmillan Publishers, 1960.
Thernstrom, Stephan and Sennett, Richard, eds. NINETEENTH-CENTURY CITIES. New Haven, CT: Yale University Press, 1969.
Wickham, E. R. CHURCH AND PEOPLE IN AN INDUSTRIAL CITY. London: Lutterworth Press, 1957.

Index

Addams, Jane, *137-38*
Alcoholism, *43, 100, 178*
Alinsky, Saul, *108-9*
Amsterdam, *12, 28, 33, 201*

Bangkok, *13, 35, 38-39, 158*
Beijing, *13, 30*
Beirut, *13, 38*
Belgrade, *60*
Berlin, *29, 38*
Boateng, Paul, *159*
Bombay, *13, 30, 37-38*
Boston, *12, 37*
Brasilia, *12, 37*
Buenos Aires, *12, 30*

Cairo, *13, 55-56, 60*
Calcutta, *13, 30, 157*
Calvin, John, *133, 152*
Cambridge, *19-20*
Caracas, *157*
Chicago, *12, 16-17, 21-27, 29, 32, 37, 46, 63-64, 73, 107-9, 129-30, 137-38, 158, 165-72;* Fairfield Avenue Baptist Church, *22, 88-106, 183*
Children, *see* Young people
Christian Laity, *130*
Church, urban, *14;* failure to evangelise, *23, 57-61;* involvement with community, *100, 102, 106-20, 155-61, 178-79;* racism in, *139-41;* types of, *131-36; see also* Mission, Roman Catholic Church
CIA, *98-100*
Clapham Sect, *20, 160*
Clergy, *see* Pastors
Clydeside, *41*
Community, caring for, *100, 102, 106-10, 155-61, 178-79;* understanding, *41-44, 111-13, 116-20*
Copenhagen, *60, 187*
Counselling, *100, 126-27, 157-58*

Daniel, *72-73*
Depression, the, *24, 43, 90*
Detroit, *12, 32*
Diognetus, Letter to, *85*
Drug abuse, *56, 60, 100, 101, 157, 170*

Education, *108, 157, 160, 164-68, 179-82, 196*
Evangelical United Front, *161*
Evangelism, *see* Mission

Family structures, *22, 36-37, 40, 104-5, 118, 125, 177-79*

House churches, *133, 134*
Housing, *22, 37, 106-7, 109, 157, 196*
Houston, *33, 43, 49*

Immigrants, *32-34, 137-38*
Industrial Revolution, *28-31*
Inner City Athletic Mission, *88*
Inter-Varsity Christian Fellowship, *17, 20*
Islam, *see* Muslims

Jakarta, *13, 30, 35*
Jesus, *63, 79-81, 158*
Jonah, *65-67*

King, Martin Luther, *18, 21, 170, 176*

Laity, *88-104, 126-27, 151-61*
Lausanne Committee for World Evangelisation, *150, 186-87*
Lausanne Covenant, *185-86*
Lewis, Elsie, *179-82*
Liverpool, *12, 32, 41*
London, *12, 28, 29, 30, 33, 38, 40-41, 53, 54-55, 141, 160-61, 179-82*
Los Angeles, *12, 30, 33*
Luther, Martin, *57, 62, 96, 101, 152*

Mafia, *25-26*

Manchester, *35*
Manila, *47*, *157-58*
Media, in evangelism, *157-58;* influence of, *32*
Mexico City, *12*, *30*, *35*, *39-40*, *60*
Miami, *12*, *26*, *32*, *33*, *50*
Mission, *144-55;* and laity, *89-104;* in multicultural society, *137-44;* programmes for, *58-59*, *95*, *151;* theology for, *62-87;* traditional, *45-51;* training for, *154-55*, *183-203*
Moody Bible Institute, *16-17*
Moses, *70-71*, *74*
Multinational companies, *34*, *38*
Mumford, Louis, *37*
Muslims, *24*, *41*, *138*, *141*

Nehemiah, *73*
Networks/Networking, *7-8*, *14*, *103-4*, *113-20*, *126-27*, *129-30*, *151-54*, *183-91*
New Delhi, *13*, *37*, *45*
New York, *12*, *29*, *30*, *32-33*, *38*, *41*, *161*
Northern Baptist Theological Seminary, *183*

Onesimus, *83-84*, *158*

Paris, *12*, *29*, *30*, *33*, *37*, *38*
Pastors, urban, allocation of time, *123-24;* co-operation with other pastors, *114-16;* failure of *53-55*, *121-23;* family life, *163-77;* financial accountability, *48*, *93;* and laity, *88-104;* pastoral teams, *125-27;* support groups, *129-30;* training of, *47*, *51-53; see also* Community, Mission
Paul, *74*, *81-84*, *158*
Political action, *24-25*, *108-10*, *117*, *158-60*, *197*
Population, mixed race of Chicago, *21-27*, *32;* shifts in, *31-41;* world, *28-30*
Purkiss, Muriel, *182*

Quito, *50*

Racism, *22*, *24-25*, *118*, *139-41*, *173-74*
Relationships, *14*, *41-44; see also* Networks/Networking

Rio de Janeiro, *12, 30*
Riots, *17, 21, 33, 35, 170*
Roman Catholic Church, *26-27, 57, 126*

San Francisco, *12, 37*
Sao Paulo, *12, 30, 37*
SCUPE, *183-85, 188*
Seattle, *12, 16, 17-18, 34, 43*
Senior citizens, *157*
Seoul, *13, 30*
Shaftesbury, Lord, *20, 160*
Shalom Ministries, *95, 130*
Shanghai, *13, 30*
Simeon, Charles, *19-21*
Singapore, *29*
Social action, *56, 76, 85, 86, 90, 100, 108-10, 155-60, 178-79, 196-98*
Social justice, *75-76, 117, 157, 160*
Spurgeon, Charles, *161*
Stockholm, *13, 34, 46*

Temple, William, *86*
Tertullian, *85*
Theology, urban, *62-87*
Tokyo-Yokohama, *13, 29, 30*
TRUST, *106, 130*

Unemployment, *18, 22, 35, 36, 37, 41, 43, 56*

Vietnam War, *22, 58-59*

Washington DC, *12, 24-25, 37, 201*
Wilberforce, William, *20, 160*
Work, *18, 24, 34, 38, 101, 152-53*
Worship, *26-27, 101-2, 145-49*

Young people, activities for, *88-89, 169-70;* in Chicago, *21-22;* as part of church family, *102, 104-5;* proportion of population, *35, 39; see also* Education, Family structures
Youth With a Mission, *46*

ECUM

Evangelical Coalition for Urban Mission

'Christians in Partnership for the Cities' – After reading Raymond Bakke's challenging book, you will want to respond to his many practical suggestions.

You may want some help from us!

We have – between us – skill, materials and people to help your ministry.

London ECUM

- events
- urban mission resources
- free quarterly mailing

Write to **Greg Smith,** Lawrence Hall, 2/4 Cumberland Road, London E13 8NH (01-476 3651)

Evangelical Christians for Racial Justice

- racial justice based on a clear biblical basis
- monitoring local and national media
- education and training events
- worship and action
- study-pack – *New Humanity*
- magazine – *Racial Justice*

Write to **Raj Patel,** ECRJ, 12 Bell Barn Shopping Centre, Cregor Street, Birmingham B15 2DZ (021-622 6807)

Frontier Youth Trust

'A missionary association of Christian youth workers'

- eight regional field officers
- training and research
- resources and materials
- events
- FYT News/Information/Updates
- a clearing house for exchanging ideas and experience in youth work

Don't be alone and unsupported in your youth ministry.

Write to **Michael Eastman,** Scripture Union House, 130 City Road, London EC1V 2NJ (01-250 1966)

Evangelical Urban Training Project

'Learning without books!'

- urban workshops
- skill training to meet your 'training need'
- training days
- eleven 'DIY' courses

Write to **Jim Hart,** EUTP, PO Box 83, Liverpool L69 8AN (051-709 1463)

Shaftesbury Project

- biblical and social education and research
- inner-city study group
- papers and study guides
- magazine – *Impact* (with newsletter – *Shaftesbury Project News*, LICC)

Write to **Roy McCloughry,** Shaftesbury Project, Old Rectory, Maid Marian Way, Nottingham NG1 6AE (0602 585731)

City Cries

– Including *ECUM Bulletin*

Stimulate your mind! Share ministries!

– three issues a year on all aspects of urban mission

– book notes

– briefing notes

Write to *City Cries*, Lawrence Hall, 2/4 Cumberland Road, London E13 8NH (01-476 3651)

What Is World Vision?

World Vision is a major Christian relief and development agency, founded over 35 years ago. World Vision now helps the hungry, the homeless, the sick and the poor in over 80 countries worldwide.

World Vision is international, interdenominational and has no political affiliation, working wherever possible through local churches and community leaders in close co-operation with the United Nations and other international relief agencies.

Childcare sponsorship is an important part of World Vision's Christian work. Over 400,000 children are currently being cared for in over 3,500 projects.

Sponsors in Europe and around the world are helping thousands of needy children by supplying food, clothing, medical care and schooling. These children usually live with their families although some are in schools or homes. Development and training are usually offered to the communities where the sponsored children live so that whole families can become self-reliant.

World Vision is able to respond with immediate and appropriate relief in crisis situations such as famines, floods, earthquakes and wars. Hundreds of thousands have been saved in Africa through feeding and medical centres. Other projects include cyclone relief for Bangladesh, relief work in Lebanon and medical assistance for Kampuchea.

Over 500 community development projects in 50 countries are helping people to help themselves towards a healthier and more stable future. These projects include agricultural and vocational training, improvements in health care and nutrition (especially for mothers and babies), instruction in hygiene, literacy classes for children and adults, development of clean water supplies and village leadership training.

World Vision's approach to aid is integrated in the sense that we believe in helping every aspect of a person's life and needs. We also help Christian leaders throughout the world to become more effective in their ministry and assist local churches in many lands with their work.

If you would like more information about the work of World Vision, please contact one of the offices listed below:

World Vision of Britain
Dychurch House
8 Abington Street
Northampton
NN1 2AJ, United Kingdom
Tel: 0604 22964

World Vision of Australia
Box 399-C, GPO
Melbourne, 3001 Victoria
Australia
Tel: 3 699 8522

World Vision Deutschland
Postfach 1848
Adenauerallee 32
D-6370 Oberusel
West Germany
Tel: 6171 56074/5/6/7

World Vision International
Christliches Hilfswerk
Mariahilferstr 10/10
A-1070 Wien
Austria
Tel: 222-961 333/366

World Vision International
Christliches Hilfswerk
Badenserstr 87
CH-8004 Zürich
Switzerland
Tel: 1-241 7222

World Vision of Ireland
17 Percy Place
Dublin 4
Eire
Tel: 01 606 058

World Vision Singapore
Maxwell Rd
PO Box 2878
Singapore 9048
Tel: 224-8037/7419

Suomen World Vision
Kalevankatu 14 C 13
00100 Helsinki 10
Finland
Tel: 90 603422

World Vision of New Zealand
PO Box 1923
Auckland
New Zealand
Tel: 9 770 879

Stichting World
Vision Nederland
Postbus 818
3800 A V Amersfoort
The Netherlands
Tel: 33 10041

World Vision Canada
6630 Turner Valley Rd
Mississauga, Ontario
Canada L5N 2S4
Tel: 416 821 3030

World Vision United States
919 West Huntington Drive
Monrovia
CA 91016
USA
Tel: 818 303 8811

World Vision of Hong Kong
PO Box 98580
Tsim Sha Tsui Post Office
Kowloon
Hong Kong
Tel: 3-7221634